ST. JOSEPH BIBLE HANDBOOK

NIHIL OBSTAT: Rev. T. Kevin Corcoran
Censor Librorum

IMPRIMATUR: ✠ Most Rev. Arthur J. Serratelli, S.T.D., S.S.L., D.D.
Bishop of Paterson

August 3, 2017

Catholic edition adapted by Catholic Book Publishing
© 2017 Catholic Book Publishing Corp.

Original edition copyright © 2014
Lion Hudson/Tim Dowley Associates

Original edition published in English under the title
The Candle Bible Handbook by Lion Hudson IP Ltd, Oxford, England

(T-649)

ISBN 978-1-941243-98-5

Printed in China
www.catholicbookpublishing.com

ST. JOSEPH
BIBLE
HANDBOOK

by Terry Jean Day & Carol J. Smith
Edited and revised by Dr. Tim Dowley

CATHOLIC BOOK PUBLISHING CORP.
New Jersey

CONTENTS

The New Testament 141

Appendix

How to Use This Book

A long, long time ago, a man took up a pen. He sat down and looked at a blank piece of paper. And he began to write, "In the beginning, God created the heavens and the earth." He wrote, and wrote, and wrote.

The first five books of the Bible are the books of Genesis through Deuteronomy. These books were not the only ones written. It took sixty-eight books, many authors, and about 1,500 years to finish the job.

This makes the Bible a bit like salad —a little of this, a little of that, all mixed in together. If you have ever flipped through the pages of a Bible, you know that it is a large, complicated, unusual book. It has all kinds of writing. It has very long and very short parts. It has a great many pages. It needs a handbook.

Bird's-eye view

This book has one purpose: to help you get a handle on the Bible. Think of being in a plane high above the ground. When you look out of the window, you can see right across the land. You are up above all the detail, where you can see the big picture. Up in the plane, you can see everything at once.

That is what this book does for you. It tells you about the key ideas in the Bible. It tells you about the main people. It gives the main points of each book in the Bible. It helps you see how all of it is put together.

Bible references

All Bible references within a chapter are from the book of the Bible covered by the chapter, unless otherwise indicated.

The Bible was originally written on papyrus scrolls.

How the Bible Is Organized

The Bible has an order to it. Each book belongs in a category.
Here is how it is all organized, from beginning to end.

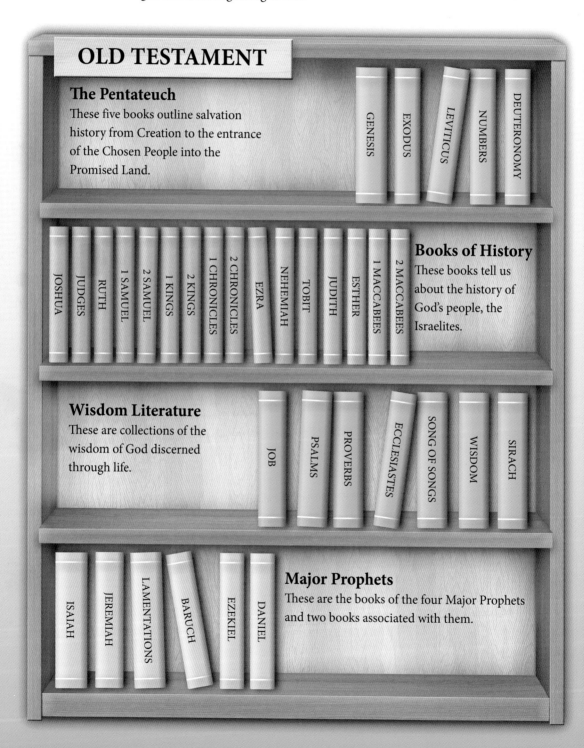

OLD TESTAMENT

The Pentateuch
These five books outline salvation
history from Creation to the entrance
of the Chosen People into the
Promised Land.

GENESIS · EXODUS · LEVITICUS · NUMBERS · DEUTERONOMY

Books of History
These books tell us
about the history of
God's people, the
Israelites.

JOSHUA · JUDGES · RUTH · 1 SAMUEL · 2 SAMUEL · 1 KINGS · 2 KINGS · 1 CHRONICLES · 2 CHRONICLES · EZRA · NEHEMIAH · TOBIT · JUDITH · ESTHER · 1 MACCABEES · 2 MACCABEES

Wisdom Literature
These are collections of the
wisdom of God discerned
through life.

JOB · PSALMS · PROVERBS · ECCLESIASTES · SONG OF SONGS · WISDOM · SIRACH

Major Prophets
These are the books of the four Major Prophets
and two books associated with them.

ISAIAH · JEREMIAH · LAMENTATIONS · BARUCH · EZEKIEL · DANIEL

Minor Prophets

The books of these prophets are shorter than those of the Major Prophets.

HOSEA · JOEL · AMOS · OBADIAH · JONAH · MICAH · NAHUM · HABAKKUK · ZEPHANIAH · HAGGAI · ZECHARIAH · MALACHI

NEW TESTAMENT

Gospels and Acts

Four Gospels, telling the Good News about Jesus, followed by the Acts of the Apostles, which tells the story of the very first Christians.

MATTHEW · MARK · LUKE · JOHN · ACTS

ROMANS · 1 CORINTHIANS · 2 CORINTHIANS · GALATIANS · EPHESIANS · PHILIPPIANS · COLOSSIANS · 1 THESSALONIANS · 2 THESSALONIANS · 1 TIMOTHY · 2 TIMOTHY · TITUS · PHILEMON · HEBREWS

Letters of Paul

These books are letters that historically have been attributed to the Apostle Paul.

Catholic Letters

These books are all the New Testament letters that are not attributed to Paul.

JAMES · 1 PETER · 2 PETER · 1 JOHN · 2 JOHN · 3 JOHN · JUDE

Apocalyptic Book

This is the only book in the New Testament written in the apocalyptic style.

REVELATION

The Old Testament

The Old Testament consists of forty-six books of different lengths and content. From the first book to the last, almost every book is different. Some books tell a story about specific people. Some give lists of rules and regulations. Some are poems. Some are sermons. God used all different kinds of people and all different kinds of writing to form the Old Testament. He did this so that we would know how we were created. He also did this to show how He has offered His friendship to us through the many years before He came to earth as Jesus to talk with us directly.

Even though Jesus is not mentioned by name in the Old Testament, the Old Testament is in many ways about Jesus. God was teaching His people to believe that the Messiah would come. The Old Testament is full of sacrifices and promises of freedom. These point to what Jesus was coming to do—to offer His life as a sacrifice and set people free from sin. The Old Testament makes many prophecies about Jesus that came true in the New Testament.

In the beginning

The Old Testament starts with the story of God's creation of the world, including people, with Adam and Eve in the Garden of Eden. By the time Noah is raising his family, though, God cannot find more than a handful of righteous people on earth. After Noah is saved from the flood in the ark, God starts again with Noah and his three sons. Later God called Abraham and made a covenant with him. He promises that Abraham will have numerous descendants, and that they will have a special relationship with God if they follow His laws. Abraham's family and descendants were called Hebrews, or Israelites. Today they are called the Jews.

Spotlight on the Jews

The rest of the Old Testament is about that family. The Israelites grow to be a whole nation of people. They are held captive in Egypt, but escape because of miracles that God performs through Moses. They wander through the desert back to their homeland, Israel. They win wars and lose wars. They obey God and then disobey Him. The last part of the Old Testament consists of oracles by the Jewish prophets, reminding them to obey God. The prophets pointed out to them that their lives were always better when they followed God's will.

Abram, later called Abraham, was living in Ur, in Mesopotamia, when he received a call from God to travel to the Promised Land.

The Middle East in Old Testament times

The Pentateuch

The first five books of the Old Testament —Genesis, Exodus, Leviticus, Numbers, and Deuteronomy—are called the Books of the Law. Genesis tells about the beginnings of the world and the beginnings of the Jewish nation. Exodus tells about the Hebrews leaving Egypt and wandering in the desert. Leviticus is a list of the rules they were to follow. Numbers is a list of who they all were and how many were in each of the twelve tribes, or families. Deuteronomy consists of Moses' words to his people before he died. It tells them how to follow God.

Books of history

Sixteen books in the Old Testament are called history books: Joshua, Judges, Ruth, 1 and 2 Samuel, 1 and 2 Kings, 1 and 2 Chronicles, Ezra, Nehemiah, Esther, Judith, Tobit, and 1 and 2 Maccabees. There are other books besides these that mention facts of history, but these books specifically tell the story of Jewish history. Joshua tells of what happened to the Hebrews after Moses died. Judges tells about wise men and women that ruled Israel. Ruth tells of a foreign woman who becomes part of Israel. 1 and 2 Samuel, 1 and 2 Kings, and 1 and 2 Chronicles tell stories of the Jewish nation and of its kings, courts, and armies. Ezra and Nehemiah tell of the return of the people to the Law of Israel. Tobit tells of a journey led by an angel. Judith tells of a Jewish woman who defeats the enemies of Israel. Esther is another story about a Jewish woman who saved her people by becoming a queen. 1 and 2 Maccabees tell of the resistance of the Jewish people to persecution.

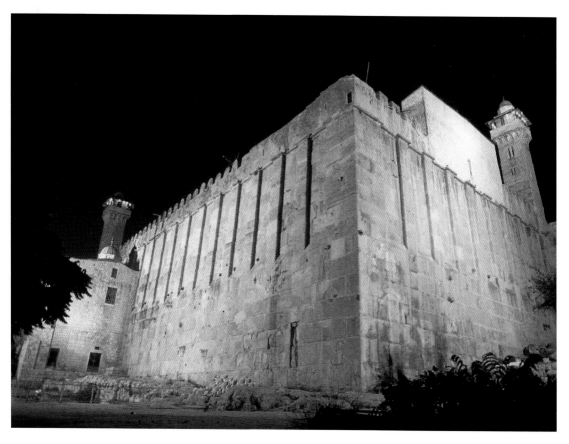

The Cave of Machpelah, Hebron, is, by tradition, the resting place of the great fathers of Israel: Abraham, Isaac, and Jacob, and their wives Sarah, Rebekah, and Leah.

Wisdom literature

Several books of the Old Testament present the wisdom of God: Job, Psalms, Proverbs, Ecclesiastes, Song of Songs, Wisdom, and Sirach. In these books, God's revelation does not come through oracles and great events as much as through a reflection upon everyday life. Many of them, although not all, are written in poetry. Using word pictures and phrases, they speak about God's wisdom, strength, and love.

Books of prophecy

The last books in the Old Testament are by prophets or preachers. The prophets reminded the Jews to obey God. The four major prophets are Isaiah, Jeremiah, Ezekiel, and Daniel. Their books and sermons are quite long and were very important to the Jewish people. There also are twelve books by minor prophets: Hosea, Joel, Amos, Obadiah, Jonah, Micah, Nahum, Habakkuk, Zephaniah, Haggai, Zechariah, and Malachi. These books are usually shorter, and we know less about these writers. What we do know is that God gave them a special commission to help their people. The Books of Lamentations and Baruch are also considered to be prophetic books.

From the beginning to the end, the Old Testament reminds us that God is our Creator, that we are to obey and worship Him, and that He would save us through His Messiah.

Old Testament Timeline

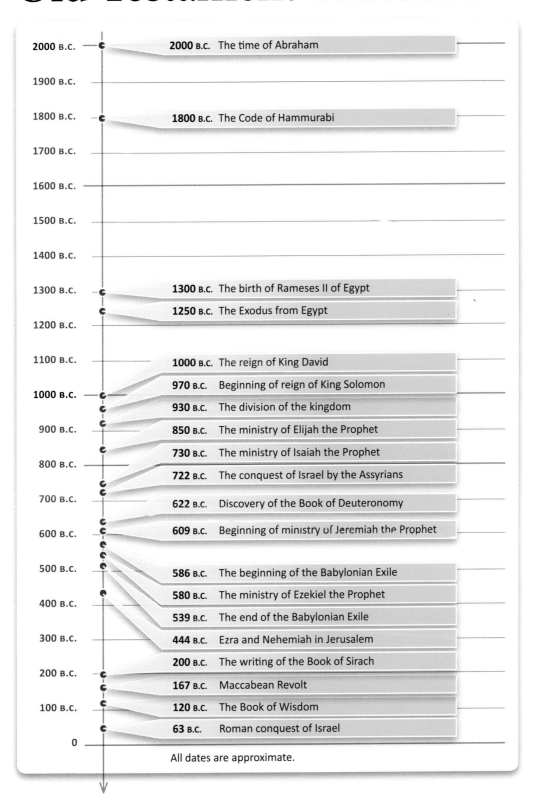

2000 B.C.	**2000 B.C.** The time of Abraham
1900 B.C.	
1800 B.C.	**1800 B.C.** The Code of Hammurabi
1700 B.C.	
1600 B.C.	
1500 B.C.	
1400 B.C.	
1300 B.C.	**1300 B.C.** The birth of Rameses II of Egypt
	1250 B.C. The Exodus from Egypt
1200 B.C.	
1100 B.C.	**1000 B.C.** The reign of King David
	970 B.C. Beginning of reign of King Solomon
1000 B.C.	**930 B.C.** The division of the kingdom
900 B.C.	**850 B.C.** The ministry of Elijah the Prophet
	730 B.C. The ministry of Isaiah the Prophet
800 B.C.	**722 B.C.** The conquest of Israel by the Assyrians
700 B.C.	**622 B.C.** Discovery of the Book of Deuteronomy
600 B.C.	**609 B.C.** Beginning of ministry of Jeremiah the Prophet
500 B.C.	**586 B.C.** The beginning of the Babylonian Exile
	580 B.C. The ministry of Ezekiel the Prophet
400 B.C.	**539 B.C.** The end of the Babylonian Exile
300 B.C.	**444 B.C.** Ezra and Nehemiah in Jerusalem
	200 B.C. The writing of the Book of Sirach
200 B.C.	**167 B.C.** Maccabean Revolt
100 B.C.	**120 B.C.** The Book of Wisdom
	63 B.C. Roman conquest of Israel
0	

All dates are approximate.

GENESIS

Genesis is the book of beginnings. It doesn't just go way back; it goes all the way back. It starts at the beginning of all beginnings. It starts at creation. It introduces us to the universe, to the earth, and to people. It introduces us to sin and to God's plans for the world. It explains what everything is and how everything began.

Genesis also introduces us to the nation of Israel. This is very important because in the Old Testament Israel is in the spotlight. God chose Israel to be His very own people. They play a part in each part of God's plans to save us from sin and win us to Himself. We can't understand the Bible without knowing about these people. Genesis lets us meet them for the first time.

By introducing us to all of that, Genesis introduces us to God. We learn Who God is and what He really wants from us. It is wondrous from start to finish.

"In the beginning God created the heavens and the earth" (1:1).

Frequently Asked Questions

Q: Is Genesis really true?
A: Yes, it is God's Word. Yet, that Word is expressed in different ways. Sometimes God's Word is expressed in historical accounts, and sometimes in parables and stories from which we can learn about God's will for us.

Q: Why did God ask Adam where he was and if he had eaten the forbidden fruit? Didn't God know?
A: God knows everything, but He wanted Adam to admit what he had done and repent.

Q: Why did God punish the world with a flood in the days of Noah?
A: There is an ancient saying: "As the sin, so the punishment." Humans had brought chaos into the world with their sins. A flood is a type of chaos, so God was simply giving people what they had asked for when they sinned.

OUTLINE

Creation (1:1—2:3)

God creates the universe and everything in it. He makes people in His own image.

Adam and Eve (2:4—5:32)

Adam and Eve have all they need, but the serpent gets them to disobey God anyway. This brings sin into the world. Cain kills his brother Abel.

Noah, the flood, and the Tower of Babel (6:1—11:32)

The world becomes so evil that God floods the whole earth. Only Noah and those on the ark with him survive.

Abraham and Sarah (12:1—25:18)

God chooses Abraham and Sarah to be the ancestors of His own people. God promises to bless the whole earth through this new people of God.

Isaac and Rebekah (25:19—28:9)

The first generation of Abraham's descendants settle in Canaan, the land God has promised them. God renews His promise to Isaac. Jacob and Rebekah trick Isaac into giving Jacob Esau's firstborn blessing.

The story of Jacob and Esau (28:10—36:43)

Jacob leaves home, and God promises to take care of him and bless him, just as He did Abraham and Isaac.

The story of Joseph (37:1—50:26)

Joseph's brothers sell him into slavery in Egypt. God, however, watches over him and soon Joseph is ruler of all Egypt, under Pharaoh. Through Joseph, God saves His people from famine as Jacob's entire family moves to Egypt.

The Ziggurat of Nanna at Ur. Ziggurats are massive temples found in Mesopotamia. The builders of the tower of Babel were probably attempting to build a structure of this kind.

KEY EVENTS
Abraham Leaves Ur

1. Ur

Ur of the Chaldeans was a thriving city with businesses and a large library. Abraham was a semi-nomadic herdsman there. When God called him to leave Ur, he had to leave all the comforts of home (11:27–32).

2. Haran

Abraham, his father, Terah, his wife, Sarah, and his nephew, Lot, set out from Ur. They followed the Tigris and Euphrates Rivers and stopped in Haran. After Terah died, Abraham continued his journey (12:1–5).

3. Canaan

From Haran, Abraham and his family journeyed to Shechem. God told Abraham He would give Canaan to Abraham's children. Abraham built an altar to God between Bethel and Ai, then he continued to the Negeb (12:6–9).

4. Egypt, Bethel

Because of a famine in Canaan, Abraham went to Egypt. Later he returned to Bethel with his wife and nephew. He had become very wealthy. Abraham and Lot now went separate ways: Lot chose the plain of Jordan and Abraham settled in Canaan (12:10—13:18).

Jacob Settles in Canaan

1. Beersheba

Jacob grew up in Beersheba but ran away from home after tricking his father, Isaac, and making Esau furious (27:42–45).

2. Bethel

Jacob stopped in Bethel, where he dreamed of angels going up and down a ladder (or staircase) to heaven. God promised him Canaan for his descendants (28:10–22). Jesus spoke of this when He promised Nathanael that he would see angels ascend and descend upon the Son of Man (John 1:51).

3. Haran

In Haran, Jacob's uncle, Laban, tricked Jacob into marrying his elder daughter, Leah. Jacob worked seven extra years before he could marry Laban's younger daughter, Rachel. After twenty years' hard work, Jacob returned to Canaan (31:36–42).

4. Canaan

Jacob was afraid of Esau and sent gifts to him. God wrestled with Jacob and changed his name to Israel. Jacob journeyed to Shechem, where he bought a piece of property and set up an altar to worship God (32:3—33:20).

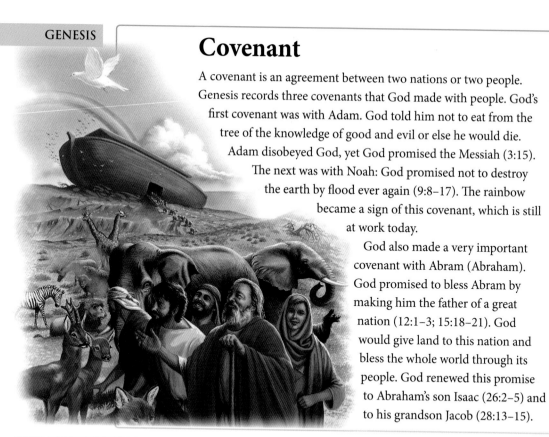

Covenant

A covenant is an agreement between two nations or two people. Genesis records three covenants that God made with people. God's first covenant was with Adam. God told him not to eat from the tree of the knowledge of good and evil or else he would die. Adam disobeyed God, yet God promised the Messiah (3:15). The next was with Noah: God promised not to destroy the earth by flood ever again (9:8–17). The rainbow became a sign of this covenant, which is still at work today.

God also made a very important covenant with Abram (Abraham). God promised to bless Abram by making him the father of a great nation (12:1–3; 15:18–21). God would give land to this nation and bless the whole world through its people. God renewed this promise to Abraham's son Isaac (26:2–5) and to his grandson Jacob (28:13–15).

Look out for...

As you read Genesis, look out for…

God's messages to people. God speaks and appears to people several times at this important time in history. Notice what He says.

Abraham. He's a very important person in the stories of Genesis. God chooses to bless the whole world through him. Abraham's name comes up again and again in the Bible.

Promises to Abraham. God promises Abraham the land and many descendants.

Joseph. All of his difficulties are a way by which God saves His people.

Study Questions

- How did people become rulers of the earth? (1:26–28)
- Why did Adam and Eve have to leave the Garden of Eden? (3:22–23)
- What did God promise Noah? (8:22)
- Why did Abram leave home and go to Canaan? (12:1–3)
- Why did God allow Joseph to suffer? (50:20)

EXODUS

OUTLINE

Israel becomes a nation (1—4)
The family of Jacob (Israel) has grown to be a whole nation. Moses is born and adopted by Pharaoh's daughter. He grows up and is told by God to rescue the Hebrews from Egypt (3:1—22).

Beginning of the rescue (5—11)
Moses returns to Egypt to tell Pharaoh to free the Israelites. God sends ten plagues to help Pharaoh make up his mind.

The Passover and Exodus (12—15)
The Angel of Death comes to Egypt. The Passover begins. The people leave Egypt. God parts the Red Sea.

Wilderness travels (16—19)
The Hebrews grow weary and start to complain, even though God is providing for them in every way.

Mount Sinai (20—23)
God gives Moses the Ten Commandments. God instructs His people.

The Tabernacle (24—40)
Moses meets with God. The people make a golden calf. Moses breaks the tablets of the Ten Commandments so they have to be written down again. The Tabernacle is constructed.

After 400 years in Egypt, the Hebrews were finally leaving. God knew all about their miserable lives as slaves. It was time to move on. He was taking them to the land He had promised to Abraham.

Exodus means departure or leaving. This book tells how God freed the Hebrews from slavery in Egypt. Pharaoh didn't want to lose his slave workers. God used ten plagues to persuade Pharaoh to let the Israelites leave, but Pharaoh had a hard heart. God protected His people from the plagues and also saved the Hebrews from drowning in the Red Sea.

The Hebrews had a lot to learn about being God's special people. For example, they did not always trust that God would provide food and water. They also made an idol and began to worship it. God, however, loved them anyway.

An Egyptian warrior

Moses and Aaron at the court of Pharaoh. After Aaron turned his staff into a snake, Pharaoh's wise men and sorcerers did the same thing by their secret arts.

Frequently Asked Questions

Q: Why did Pharaoh like Joseph and his family but make slaves of the Israelites?

A: The pharaoh who knew Joseph was different from the pharaoh who enslaved the Israelites. 400 years had passed. During that time, the Israelites had become very numerous. This pharaoh feared they would fight him.

Q: Why did God send plagues on Egypt?

A: Egyptians had many false gods. The Lord showed His power against these false gods with each of the plagues.

Q: Why did the Israelites complain after they left Egypt?

A: The Israelites missed the Egyptian food and were afraid they couldn't get water.

Look out for...

As you read Exodus, look out for...

Distrust. Over and over again, the people fail to trust God, even though He takes care of them.

Signs. God gives the Hebrews many signs to help them believe.

Miracles. Throughout Exodus, God works many miracles and wonders.

Q: What were the Israelites doing while God was giving the Ten Commandments to Moses?

A: They became impatient for Moses to return, made a golden calf as an idol, and began to worship it.

In the Desert of Sinai, Moses climbed Mount Sinai, where God gave him the Ten Commandments.

Plagues

A plague is something so terrible that it affects everyone around. God used ten different plagues to persuade Pharaoh to release the Israelites. Small groups of locusts, frogs, and flies can occur in nature; yet when swarms of them appear all at once, it's considered a plague. Egypt had more than just a few thousand flies: there were millions of flies everywhere. God used these ten plagues to show His power to Pharaoh. Still, Pharaoh did not listen (7:14—12:30).

Study Questions

- What orders did Pharaoh give the Hebrew midwives? (1:15–16)
- What did the midwives do? (1:17–21)
- How did Moses' mother not quite obey Pharaoh? (1:22—2:4)
- How did God get Moses' attention? (3:1–6)
- How did blood save the Israelites? (12:21–30)
- How did God lead the Israelites out of Egypt? (13:20–22)
- In what ways did God fight the Egyptians as they chased the Israelites? (14:21–31)
- What were some of the laws that God gave the Israelites? (23:1–9)

KEY EVENTS

MEDITERRANEAN SEA

Shechem

Jericho

Mt. Nebo

CANAAN

Hebron

Gaza

Valley of Eshcol

MOAB

Rameses

Succoth

R. Nile

Kadesh

SINAI

Elath

EGYPT

Elim

Hazeroth

MIDIAN

Rephidim

Mt. Sinai

- - - *Route of twelve spies*

■■■ *Route of Israelites*

RED SEA

N

Moses carries two stone tablets on which are written the Ten Commandments.

The Exodus

1. Elim and Rephidim

Moses crossed the Red Sea, then led his people south. The desert was hot and dry, but God provided water and food and helped the Israelites defeat their enemy, the Amalekites (14:21–25; 16:1, 13–15; 17:1–15).

2. Mount Sinai

For almost a year, the Israelites camped at the foot of Mount Sinai. God gave them the Ten Commandments and the plan for the Tabernacle (19—40).

3. Kadesh

Spies went into the Promised Land, but ten of the twelve gave a discouraging report. The people were frightened and wouldn't obey God's command to enter. God made them wander in the desert for forty years (Numbers 13—14).

4. Jericho

Moses died on Mount Nebo. Joshua led the people across the Jordan River on dry land, defeated Jericho, and began to take Canaan (Joshua 1—6).

LEVITICUS

OUTLINE

The system of sacrifices and the priests (1—10)
Notes on how to offer sacrifices. The priests begin their work.

Laws of sanitation and health (11—15)
Notes on how to keep themselves and their camp clean.

The annual atonement (16—17)
Notes on how to celebrate the yearly Day of Atonement.

Holy living (18—22)
Notes on actions that greatly displease God. Also many laws and rules.

The priests, their services, and their duties (23—24)
Notes on the feasts and special days, called holydays, and the role of the priests in the celebrations.

Special years; warnings and blessings; vows and tithes (25—27)
Notes on traditions the people should keep, such as the Sabbath Year and the Year of Jubilee. There also is a pledge that there will be blessings for obedience and punishments for disobedience.

Making the Israelites into a special nation took a great deal of work. God had to teach His people a whole new way of life. Therefore, in the Book of Leviticus He gave them numerous instructions on how to live and how to worship.

Leviticus was a handbook for the Hebrew priests. It taught about the sacrifices God wanted people to offer for forgiveness. It also was a guide for holy living. Leviticus mentions holiness many times. A special verse says, "Be holy, for I am holy. I am the LORD, your God" (19:2).

God gave clear directions for worship. Two of Aaron's sons disobeyed these rules. Their disobedience was such a serious matter that they died. The offerings described in Leviticus help us understand why Jesus came and died.

The high priest wore a breastplate with twelve precious stones. Each stone represented one of the tribes of Israel.

Priests make a burnt offering on the great altar that stood in front of the Israelite Tabernacle. The priest in the foreground is blowing a shofar, a ram's-horn trumpet.

Passover Lamb

In the final plague on Egypt, the oldest son of every household died unless lamb's blood was smeared on the frame of the door of the house. The Israelites smeared their doorposts, and the Angel of Death "passed over." From then on, they celebrated this "Passover" with a special meal each year at the same time (23:2, 4–5).

This meal reminded them of God's rescue; it also teaches us about the work Jesus would do. When Jesus died on the Cross, He became our Passover Lamb and saved us from death (John 1:29, 36).

Frequently Asked Questions

Q: Why did the people have to sacrifice animals?

A: God wanted the people to understand how serious sin is.

Q: What kind of animals did God want as offerings?

A: The offerings God wanted were bulls, lambs, goats, doves, and pigeons, depending on the occasion. The offering always had to be a perfect animal. It had to be the best—not an animal with a blemish or a disease.

Q: Why did the people have to keep on offering sacrifices?

A: These sacrifices did not really take away sin; they made amends for offending God. People sin again and again, so before Jesus came, people had to offer sacrifices again and again. Jesus' death on the Cross destroyed sin; His sacrifice for sin was needed only once.

Look out for...

As you read Leviticus, look out for...

Holiness. *This whole book is about holiness. Over and over again, God teaches His people to be holy.*

Priests. *This book is like a manual for priests. Because of this, you will find numerous references to priests.*

Sacrifices. *Sacrifices were to be an important part of Jewish worship. The first part of Leviticus tells how these sacrifices were to be made.*

Feasts and holydays. *God uses the Jewish feasts and holydays to remind the people of the miracles He has performed among them, just as Christmas reminds us of Jesus' birth.*

Study Questions

- How did Aaron and the priests know God cared about holiness? (10:1–11)
- What sacrifice would a poor person make after the birth of a child? (12:6)
- Why was it forbidden to eat blood? (17:11)
- How often was the Jubilee Year celebrated? (25:8)
- What rewards did God promise the Israelites if they obeyed Him? (26:1–13)
- What did God say to the people who did not want to obey Him? (26:14–17)
- How do we know the Book of Leviticus is important? (27:34)

The Tabernacle Tent

While the Israelites were wandering in the desert, they took with them a movable tent of meeting or Tabernacle (Numbers 11:16). They put up this tent in the middle of their camp. The Tabernacle area was enclosed by curtains hung on wooden pillars. The Tabernacle tent consisted of two parts. The larger front space was called the Holy Place and housed the altar of incense, the golden lampstand, and the table for the bread of the Presence. The smaller, back space was called the Most Holy Place, or Holy of Holies, and housed the Ark of the Covenant. Only the high priest entered this area only once a year, on the Day of Atonement. In front of the Tabernacle tent stood a laver for ritual washing and the great altar of sacrifice.

NUMBERS

After all that God did in Egypt to prove He was God, the people of Israel still doubted Him. The Book of Numbers tells about the test of faith they faced.

The book gets its name from the fact that the people of Israel were numbered, or counted, twice. The first time they were counted was soon after they had left Egypt. God wanted Moses to know how many fighting men he had. The people grumbled and complained and didn't believe God could take them into the Promised Land.

Moses sent twelve spies to see how best they should conquer that land. When they returned, ten said it was impossible. Only two—Joshua and Caleb—said, yes, there were giants; yes, it was a big job; but yes, the Lord would give them the victory as He had said. The people listened to the ten frightened men and refused to go into battle.

Because they doubted, they spent forty years wandering in the desert. None of the people who doubted God lived to see His promise fulfilled.

At the end of this long, winding trip, Moses counted the people again.

"The Lord spoke to Moses, saying, 'Send some men out to explore the land of Canaan that I am giving to the people of Israel. Send one of the leaders from each of the ancestral tribes'" (13:1–2, NCV).

OUTLINE

Numbering and organizing the people (1—5)

Moses and Aaron count the people of Israel for the first time and begin to give certain jobs to certain tribes.

Preparing for the journey (6—10)

The people get ready to travel by offering sacrifices and celebrating their first Passover in freedom.

Marching to Kadesh (11—12)

The people complain because the trip is so difficult. Some even wish they were back in Egypt. God provides for them by sending quail to eat.

God sent the people quail to eat.

The twelve spies (13—14)

Spies explore the land. Only two report that the land can be conquered. The other ten report that it would be impossible for them to defeat their enemies there. The people become frightened and disturbed. Once again, they don't trust God. The two spies who trusted were the only ones allowed to enter the Promised Land.

More lack of faith (15—21)

The people rebel against Moses. God uses an earthquake to punish them. Aaron's family begins to act as priests when a walking stick starts to bud as if it were a living plant.

Balaam's prophecy and a problem with the kingdom of Moab (22—25)

Balaam comes to curse Israel, but blesses it instead. His own donkey talks to him. Then the Israelites get tricked by people who worship idols.

Another count, a new ruler, more rules (26—36)

The people of Israel are counted a second time. Joshua becomes the next leader of the Israelites. Two tribes receive their portion of land because they want to settle before crossing the River Jordan.

The Israelites Journey to the Promised Land

MEDITERRANEAN SEA

Jericho
Mt. Nebo
Hebron
Gaza
Valley of Eshcol
CANAAN
MOAB
Rameses
GOSHEN
Kadesh
R. Nile
SINAI
Elath
EGYPT
Elim
Hazeroth
MIDIAN
Rephidim
Mt. Sinai

- - - *Journey of spies*
- - - Journey of Israelites

RED SEA

N

During their long years in the desert, the Israelites lived in tents.

Frequently Asked Questions

Q: Why were the people counted?
A: Men who were twenty years or older were counted so they could serve in the army.

Q: Since the camp for the Israelites was very large, how did Moses tell the people they were to move on?
A: God told Moses to make two silver trumpets to call the people together and move camp.

Q: Why were Miriam and Aaron jealous of their brother, Moses?
A: They, too, wanted to be important leaders.

Q: Why didn't ten of the spies want to enter Canaan?
A: The spies thought the people of Canaan were so large that they felt like grasshoppers by comparison, and they were afraid.

Look out for...

As you read Numbers, look out for...

Rules and regulations. *Numbers gives many guidelines–especially for priests—on how to do things.*

Lack of faith. *The people of God keep losing their faith even though God has provided for them.*

Counting. *The whole Hebrew nation is counted twice.*

Study Questions

- How did God guide the people from place to place? (9:15–23)
- What was manna like? (11:7–9)
- Why did Moses lose the chance to enter the Promised Land? (20:2–12)
- What did Balaam's donkey do when he was on his way to curse the Israelites? (22:21-33)
- Before he died, what did Moses ask God to do? (27:12–23)
- What was a city of refuge? (35:9–15)

DEUTERONOMY

OUTLINE

Story of the journey (1—5)

The Hebrews leave Mount Sinai, where they received the Ten Commandments. Moses appoints leaders for each tribe. The people wander through the desert and fight battles.

Rules and regulations (5—26)

Moses reviews the Ten Commandments and many other rules for living.

Curses and blessings (27—30)

Moses reminds the people that they will receive blessings for obedience and curses for disobedience.

Moses' successor (31—34)

Joshua becomes the leader of the Israelites and Moses says goodbye to his people. Moses dies in the land of Moab and never enters the Promised Land.

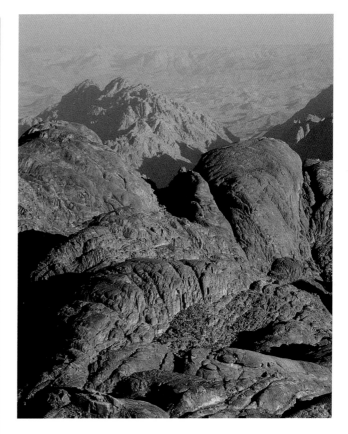

The bare slopes of Mount Sinai, where Moses received the Ten Commandments.

Deuteronomy is a book of memories, like a scrapbook. Moses had spent forty years taking the Israelites on a journey that was supposed to have taken only two years. The people who disobeyed God all died without seeing the Promised Land. Now, the people who came after them were about to enter Canaan.

Moses reminded them of all that God had done for them over the past forty years. He repeated the Law. He told them to believe God and do His will.

Moses reminded the people that they had to choose between two paths: obedience to God's Law, which would lead to reward, and disobedience to that Law, which would lead to punishment and death. Moses also blessed the people. He then made Joshua their new leader.

Deuteronomy is the fifth Book of the Law. Jesus knew it well; it is the book He quoted when Satan tried to tempt Him to disobey His Father.

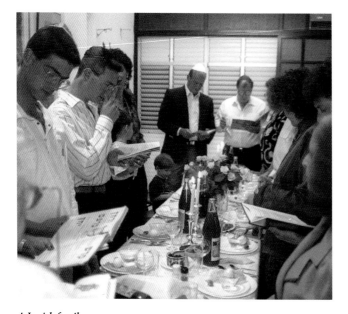

A Jewish family remembers the deliverance from Egypt in the annual festival of Passover.

A special Seder plate and cup, used at Passover

Look out for...

As you read Deuteronomy, look out for...

The Ten Commandments. This book retells some of the stories from Exodus, including how God gave Moses the Ten Commandments.

God's faithfulness. Even when the Hebrews do not have much faith, God faithfully takes care of them.

What God requires. God tells the people clearly what He wants: their worship, love, and obedience.

Celebrations. God does not just give His people rules; He also tells them to hold festivals to remind them of the good things He has done.

Frequently Asked Questions

Q: Why wasn't Moses allowed to enter the Promised Land?
A: Moses had not trusted in God's promise when he struck the rock to find water for the people.

Q: Why was Moses afraid the people would forget God?
A: Moses knew that when the people had plenty of food and an easy life they might forget to trust God.

Q: How did God take care of His people in the desert?
A: God sent bread from heaven called "manna" and water for them to drink. Also, their sandals did not wear out for forty years!

The view from Mount Nebo, Jordan

The Promised Land

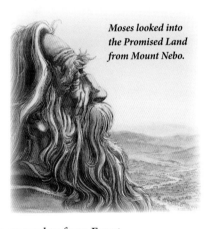

Moses looked into the Promised Land from Mount Nebo.

Many years before the Exodus from Egypt, God had promised Abraham some land. We know that land today as Israel. When people speak of going to the Holy Land, they mean the land where Jesus grew up. It is the same land that God promised to Abraham and that the Hebrews journeyed to from Egypt.

Deuteronomy describes the time just before the nation first entered the Promised Land. In this book, they are just across the river from this land. Moses goes to the top of the mountain to look across and see the land that is theirs. This land has always been, and always will be, important to the Jewish people (34:1–4).

Study Questions

- What are the Ten Commandments? (5:6–21)
- What is one reason that God wants people to obey Him with all their heart? (5:29)
- How did God say parents should teach their children God's laws? (6:6–9)
- Before Moses died, what was so important about the advice he gave Joshua? (31:7–8)
- What was Moses like at the end of his life? (34:7)
- How was Moses special? (34:10–12)

JOSHUA

The Israelites cross the River Jordan and finally enter the Promised Land. The priests carry the Ark of the Covenant on their shoulders.

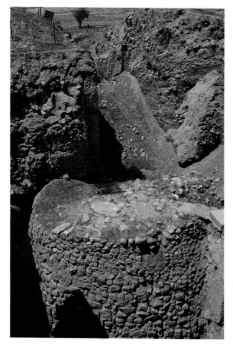

Archaeologists have discovered many ancient remains at the site of the city of Jericho.

The Israelites needed a strong leader to take them into the Promised Land. Joshua took up where Moses left off. Finally, the people were ready to follow God's plan. It may have seemed a strange plan, but it worked. The Book of Joshua tells about the battles the Israelites had in taking the land that God had given them.

God dried up the waters of the River Jordan so the Israelites could cross into the Promised Land on dry ground (just as He had dried up the waters of the Red Sea in the Exodus). Marching around a city doesn't sound like the way to win a battle, but the Israelites obeyed God. Once each day for six days, they marched around Jericho. On the seventh day, they marched around seven times. The seventh time, Joshua told the people to shout. They shouted and the walls of Jericho came crashing down.

This was just the beginning of conquering the land God had promised to Abraham, Isaac, and Jacob. Sometimes, the people disobeyed, and then they failed. But God took them into Canaan and gave each tribe a new home.

Joshua's instructions to the people are also found in this book. Like Moses, Joshua wanted his people to obey God and enjoy His blessings.

OUTLINE

Joshua becomes leader (1)

God tells Joshua how to be successful. Joshua takes charge of the people and begins to lead.

Taking over Canaan (2—12)

Some spies go to Jericho and are taken care of by a woman named Rahab. God parts the River Jordan for all the people to cross. The people circle Jericho and the walls fall down. Rahab and her family are spared. She becomes an ancestor of King David and Jesus.

Dividing and settling the land (13—22)

The people occupy the land and continue to fight the few people who will not let them settle in peace.

Joshua says goodbye (23—24)

Joshua gives a final, inspiring speech. He reminds the people of everything God has done for them.

Frequently Asked Questions

Q: What made Joshua brave enough to take Moses' place?
A: God told Joshua He would be with him wherever he went.

Q: Why did Rahab hide the Israelite spies from her own people?
A: Rahab had heard about God's power, and she decided to follow Him instead of her people's false gods.

Q: How did the Israelites know which people were on their side?
A: Rahab put a red cord in the window of her house. Everyone inside the house was saved.

Q: How did the Israelites defeat great Jericho easily, but were themselves defeated by the little town of Ai?
A: Achan had hidden some treasures in his tent, against God's instructions. All the Israelites suffered for his selfishness by losing the battle against Ai.

On the seventh day of marching around Jericho, the priests blew their trumpets, the Israelites shouted, and the great walls collapsed.

Tribes

After the land had been taken, it was divided among the tribes. These are large family units—not just parents and children, but all their distant relatives, too. A tribe starts with the parents' parents and the grandparents' parents and traces its roots back to one person.

The tribes of Israel are named after ten of Jacob's sons and two of his grandsons. (Jacob was Abraham's grandson. God promised Abraham that his descendants would be as many as the stars in the sky.) Whenever the Book of Joshua talks about a tribe, it means the families that came from one of those sons or grandsons. Every tribe, except the tribe of Levi, received some land. Levi is the tribe from which Moses and his family came. This tribe became priests, leaders of worship, and caretakers of the Temple. Because they worked in the Temple, they did not need land.

The twelve tribes

Reuben	Asher
Simeon	Issachar
Judah	Zebulun
Dan	Benjamin
Naphtali	Manasseh*
Gad	Ephraim*

*Manasseh and Ephraim were sons of Joseph.

Look out for...

As you read Joshua, look out for...

Battles. There are many important and miraculous battles.

Good leadership. Joshua is a strong leader who takes good care of God's people.

Wins and losses. When the people obey and trust God, the battles go well; when they do not, they meet with far less success.

Miracles. God keeps performing miracles for His people. The sun stands still, the waters part, and many other miracles take place.

Study Questions

- What made Rahab want to help the Israelite spies? (2:8–13)
- Why did Joshua set up twelve stones at Gilgal? (4:19–24)
- How did Joshua make sure the people knew what God expected and what He promised? (8:30–35)
- How did the people of Gibeon trick Joshua? (9:1–27)
- How did Joshua gain extra daylight hours to win a battle? (10:9–14)
- How did God keep His promises to the Israelites? (21:43–45)

KEY EVENTS
The Conquest of Canaan

1. River Jordan

The priests carried the Ark of the Covenant into the River Jordan. The water stopped flowing and everyone crossed into the Promised Land on dry ground (2:1—4:24). Once in the Promised Land, they camped at Gilgal and celebrated Passover (5:13—6:5).

2. Jericho and Ai

Joshua and the people obeyed God and broke down the walls of Jericho by marching around the city (6:1—27). Because of Achan's sin, the Israelites were unable to take the next city, Ai. After dealing with Achan, they captured Ai (7:1—8:29).

3. Mount Ebal and Mount Gerizim

Joshua, the priests, and the people renewed their covenant with God (8:30–35).

4. Gibeon

Five kings attacked the city of Gibeon, which had made a treaty with the Israelites. Joshua and his troops joined the battle. It lasted all day, and Joshua asked God to make the sun stand still until the Israelites defeated the enemy (10:1–43).

The Israelites advance into Canaan

Five Canaanite kings attack Gibeon

Five kings defeated and flee

N

5. Hazor

Another group of kings joined together to fight Israel. God, however, gave His people the victory (11:1–23).

6. Shiloh

Many of the enemy armies were defeated, and the Israelites enjoyed a time of peace. They gathered in Shiloh and set up the Tabernacle to worship God (18:1—19:51). This is where the judge Samuel first served the Lord (1 Samuel 3).

JUDGES

Gideon defeats the Midianites with a tiny force of 300 men, equipped with burning torches and trumpets (Chapter 7).

The great leaders Moses and Joshua were dead. The Israelites had seen God keep His promise to take them into the Promised Land. They, however, became lazy about obeying God. They didn't remove the sinful people who lived in Canaan. Instead, the Israelites copied the ways of their enemies. The Book of Judges tells of the trouble and sorrow the Israelites went through.

The people of Israel married people who had idols as gods. Soon the Israelites themselves turned to these false gods. God punished them for turning their backs on Him. Instead of enjoying the good things of the Promised Land, the Israelites suffered war, slavery, and hardship. When they cried to God for help, He sent a judge to lead them into battle and bring them back to Himself.

Again and again, the Israelites forgot their promise to obey God. So, again and again, He allowed their enemies to defeat them. The Israelites would then be sorry for their sins and ask Him to save them, and God would send another judge to help them.

For about 325 years, this pattern continued. God used thirteen men and women to judge and help His people. The judges were not perfect, but they followed God's leadership. He used them to help His people.

OUTLINE

Introduction (1—2)
The Hebrews do not conquer all of the Promised Land. This means some of their enemies are left to cause them difficulty. It's these enemies that the judges have to fight.

Israel's first judges (3)
Othniel, Ehud, and Shamgar serve as Israel's judges.

Sisera is defeated (4—5)
Deborah defends Israel with Barak's help and defeats Sisera.

Gideon defends Israel (6—10)
Gideon, Abimelech, Tola, and Jair serve as judges. Gideon defeats the Midianites with a small army.

Jephthah defends Israel (11—12)
Jephthah, Ibzan, Elon, and Abdon serve as judges.

Samson (13—16)
God makes Samson especially strong to defend Israel, but he is betrayed by Delilah.

Israel without a leader (17—21)
This is a time of much confusion in the life of God's people.

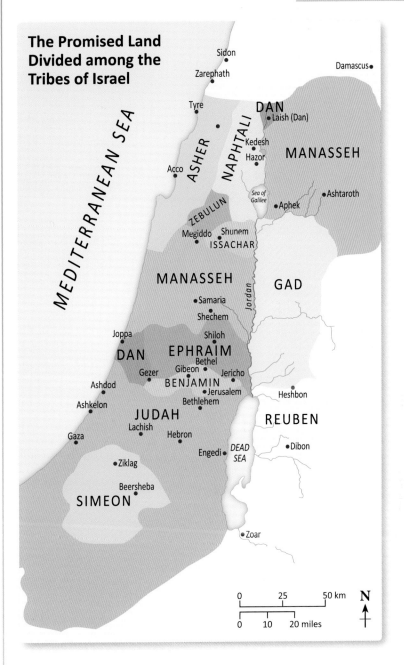

The Promised Land Divided among the Tribes of Israel

Samson and Delilah. Samson once killed a thousand Philistines with a donkey's jawbone.

Nazirites

Nazirites were people who kept strict religious laws. A person could be a Nazirite for his or her whole life, or for just a short time. Nazirites did not drink wine or eat grapes. This showed they were willing to give up something enjoyable to serve God. Also, they never cut their hair or used a razor. Three well-known characters from the Bible were Nazirites for life: Samson, Samuel, and John the Baptist (Judges 13; 1 Samuel 1; Luke 1:11–17).

Study Questions

- Why did Othniel become the first judge of Israel? (3:7–11)
- Why did God give glory to a woman and not to General Barak? (4:9)
- What sign did God give Gideon to show that He was about to deliver His people? (6:36-40)
- How did Samson defeat the Philistines even though he was blind and weak? (16:25-30)
- What went wrong with Israel during the time of the judges? (21:25)

Look out for...

As you read Judges, look out for...

Falling away. *Israel goes through patterns of following God, then falling away from Him.*

Revival. *Good, strong judges help bring Israel back to God.*

Rebellion. *Whenever the Israelites turn away from God, they lead evil, violent lives.*

Frequently Asked Questions

Q: Why didn't God keep His promise to help His people?
A: God promised to bless the Israelites if they obeyed Him. When they disobeyed, He stopped helping them. Yet, He still sent judges who were able to defend Israel from its enemies.

Q: Who were judges?
A: Judges were leaders God called to help the Israelites. They showed the people their wrongdoing, encouraged them, led them in battle, and brought them back to God. Sometimes they ruled foolishly.

Q: Who were the greatest judges?
A: Most people think Gideon, Deborah, and Samson were the greatest judges.

RUTH

It was a dark time in the history of the Israelites. Everyone was doing what he or she wanted. Very few people were trying to obey God. Few people thought of helping others. In this unhappy time, there lived three people whose lives were different; their story is told in the Book of Ruth.

Naomi, Ruth, and Boaz did not just think of themselves. They thought about what would be good for others and helped those in need. They also loved God.

Ruth was a widow. She lived in the land of Moab with her mother-in-law, Naomi. Naomi was a widow, too. Naomi wanted to return to Bethlehem in Judah. She told Ruth to stay in Moab and go back to her people. Ruth, however, loved her mother-in-law. Ruth promised to go with Naomi and take care of her. She also wanted to worship the true God.

When Naomi and Ruth arrived in Bethlehem, Ruth worked to get food for them. Boaz was kind and told Ruth she could collect grain in his fields. In the end, Boaz married Ruth. He and Ruth then took care of Naomi together.

The Book of Ruth shows that no matter how bad things are, there are always some people who love God.

Ruth Travels from Moab to Bethlehem

Jericho

Bethlehem

DEAD SEA

JUDAH

MOAB

OUTLINE

Naomi in Moab (1)
Naomi's husband and sons die, and she decides to move back to Bethlehem. One of her daughters-in-law, Ruth, goes with her.

Ruth meets Boaz (2)
Ruth gathers wheat in a field owned by Boaz. Boaz is nearly Naomi's closest relative in town.

Ruth asks Boaz to take care of her (3)
According to Jewish law, a relative such as Boaz could marry Ruth and take care of her. Ruth asks him to do so.

Boaz marries Ruth (4)
Ruth and Boaz marry and have a son who is the grandfather of King David.

The rich farmer Boaz saw poor Ruth gathering leftover grain in his field.

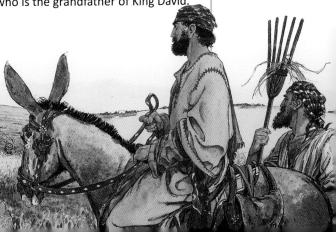

Look out for...

As you read Ruth, look out for...

Loyalty. *Ruth shows loyalty to Naomi by leaving her own homeland to be with her mother-in-law.*

Relationships. *This story is all about the relationships between Naomi and Ruth; Ruth and Boaz; and Ruth, Boaz, and their son.*

Courage. *Ruth, Naomi, and Boaz all show courage.*

Frequently Asked Questions

Q: Why were Naomi and her family in Moab?

A: There had been a famine in Judah. Naomi, her husband, and her two sons went to Moab to find food.

Q: Why did Naomi need Ruth to take care of her?

A: In her day, widows were treated badly or ignored. They became poor and had little unless a family member helped them.

Ruth and Boaz married and had a son. David was among their descendants.

Study Questions

- Why did Naomi agree to let Ruth go with her to Bethlehem? (1:15–18)
- What did Boaz hear about Ruth? (2:11–12)
- What kind of man was Boaz? (2:19–20)
- How did God bless Ruth, Boaz, and Naomi? (4:13–17)

1 SAMUEL

The first Book of Samuel is named after the man who was last, first, and best—all rolled into one. Samuel was the last judge of Israel. He was the first prophet after Moses. He also was one of the best prophets of Israel. Besides all that, Samuel was a priest.

During Samuel's leadership, the people of Israel decided that they wanted to have a king like all of the nations that surrounded them. Samuel tried to tell them of the problems and trouble they would have if they had a king. The people would not listen. They wanted a king anyway. Although it was not His first choice for them, God did let the people have a king.

Saul became the first king of the Israelites. Samuel was the priest who anointed him. In Old Testament times, when a king was appointed, it was the custom for a priest to pour oil on his head. This anointing was a sign that God had chosen him, and that God had poured His spirit on him.

This historical book of Israel records Saul's promising start, his disobedience to God, and his final failure. Other important stories of Israel in 1 Samuel are David and Goliath, David's friendship with Jonathan, Saul's attempts to kill David, and the death of Saul.

Samuel visited Jesse to find a king to succeed Saul. God showed him that of all Jesse's sons, David, the young shepherd boy, was the chosen one. Samuel is depicted anointing David.

Saul's royal palace was at Gibeah, just north of Jerusalem.

OUTLINE

Samuel as a child and a judge (1—8)

Hannah prays for a child and God gives her Samuel. Samuel grows up in the Temple and becomes a great prophet. The Israelites ask for a king, and Samuel warns them of the dangers in following a man instead of God.

Saul's rise to power (9—14)

Samuel anoints Saul as Israel's first king. Saul wins some victories but also makes mistakes.

Saul's decline and his struggles with David (15—31)

Saul begins to fail as a leader. Samuel anoints David as future king, and David kills Goliath. At first, Saul liked David, and Saul's son Jonathan is David's best friend. Saul then becomes jealous of David because the people speak of David as a great leader. By the time of Saul's death, Saul sees David as an enemy.

Frequently Asked Questions

Q: How could Samuel have so many important functions?

A: Samuel's mother, Hannah, asked God for a son. She promised to give him back to God to serve Him. Since his childhood, Samuel was training to serve God. God was able to use him in many ways.

Q: Why did the Israelites want a king?

A: Samuel was getting old, and his sons did not follow his good example. Since they were very bad leaders, the people used this as an excuse to have a king.

Q: What kind of man was Saul?

A: Saul was tall and handsome, the son of a wealthy man. He was humble at first, but later he became proud and jealous of David. He also began to pick and choose when he would obey God.

KEY EVENTS
The Formation of the Kingdom of Israel

1. Ramah

Saul was looking for his father's lost donkeys. He didn't know the prophet Samuel was waiting for him at his home in Ramah. The people wanted a king, and God told Samuel to anoint Saul as king of Israel (7:15–17; 9:3—10:1).

2. Jabesh-gilead

The people of Jabesh-gilead were besieged and asked Saul for help. Saul gathered an army and rescued them. The people celebrated by going to Gilgal to worship God and confirmed Saul as their new king (11:1–15).

3. Elah

Saul gathered his army in the valley of Elah to fight the Philistines. The giant Goliath mocked them and challenged any one Israelite to a fight. David accepted the challenge and killed Goliath with his shepherd's sling and a stone. The Philistines fled, but they were pursued by the Israelites. From then on, David helped Saul to defeat their enemies and became very popular (17:1—18:5).

4. Hebron

King Saul was jealous of David because the people loved him. For years, Saul chased David and tried to kill him. Then Saul was killed in battle by the Philistines. The people of Hebron made David king of Judah (2 Samuel 2:4).

5. Jerusalem

Seven-and-a-half years after Saul's death, David became king over all the tribes of Israel and made Jerusalem his capital (2 Samuel 5:4–7).

Philistines

The Philistine people lived on the coastal plains of Palestine. We may even have gotten the word Palestine from the word Philistine.

These people were more advanced than the Hebrews. They already worked with metal in a way the Hebrews did not. This gave the Philistines an advantage in battle. Perhaps the most famous Philistine was Goliath. But Goliath, for all his might and metal, was killed by a shepherd boy with a sling, showing that when God is on your side, anything can happen (6:17–18; 13:19–23).

Philistine warriors had a distinctive headdress. The Philistines had an advantage over the Israelites because they were able to make iron weapons.

Look out for...

As you read 1 Samuel, look out for...

Saul. *Sometimes Saul follows God; other times he definitely does not.*

Faithful friendships. *Jonathan's and David's friendship teaches us how to be good friends.*

Study Questions

• What was so bad about having a king in Israel? (8:10–20)
• What did Saul do that made God take away his kingdom? (13:7–14)
• How did Saul's servants describe David? (16:18–19)
• Why were King Saul and his soldiers afraid of Goliath? (17:4–11)
• Why didn't David kill King Saul when he had the chance? (26:5–11)

2 SAMUEL

OUTLINE

David becomes king (1—10)

David officially becomes king. Even though Saul tried to kill David, David respects the memory of Saul and his son Jonathan. David transfers the Ark of the Covenant to Jerusalem.

David's sin (11—18)

David sins with Bathsheba, another man's wife. He then has her husband killed in battle. His life is never the same, as he and his family have to live with the results of what he has done. David's son Absalom plots against him, and David flees from Jerusalem.

David restores his kingdom (19—24)

David has a small band of mighty men who show their loyalty over and over again. Unfortunately, David counts the men of Israel in preparation for war and lets the numbers go to his head. God disciplines him for his sin of pride.

David's life was so important to Israel that the whole second Book of Samuel is filled with stories about him.

Most people would expect that David would have been glad when King Saul was finally killed in battle. David, however, mourned for his king and for his friend Jonathan.

The second Book of Samuel tells how David became king over Judah and then over all of Israel. Since David followed God's ways in ruling his people, God made David successful. His people loved him and were devoted to him.

David was a good king and military leader, but he made mistakes as a father. Sometimes he did not discipline his children well, which caused him much grief.

David was far from perfect. He committed the serious sins of adultery, deceit, and murder. When the prophet Nathan told David he was guilty, King David admitted his sin and repented. God forgave David, but 2 Samuel records the lifelong consequences that David and his family suffered.

King David was a skilled musician.

How the city wall was breached

David first made Jerusalem the capital of Israel. He captured the city from the Jebusites by surprise.

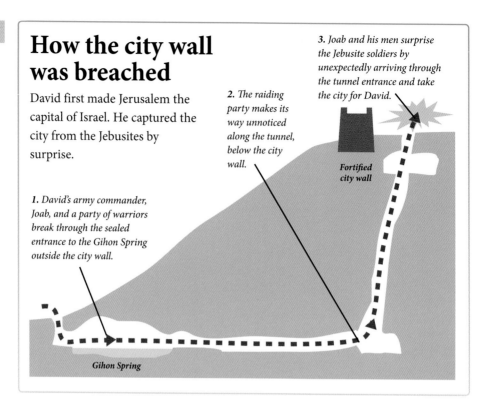

2. The raiding party makes its way unnoticed along the tunnel, below the city wall.

3. Joab and his men surprise the Jebusite soldiers by unexpectedly arriving through the tunnel entrance and take the city for David.

Fortified city wall

1. David's army commander, Joab, and a party of warriors break through the sealed entrance to the Gihon Spring outside the city wall.

Gihon Spring

David's Kingdom

Frequently Asked Questions

Q: How do we know that David was sorry that King Saul was killed?
A: David mourned and fasted because of his grief. He also wrote a lament about King Saul and Jonathan.

Q: What happened to King Saul's family?
A: David was kind to Jonathan's son Mephibosheth. He gave Mephibosheth all Saul's land and let him eat at the king's table.

Q: If David was sorry for his sin, why did God still punish him?
A: God does not take sin lightly. Most of the time sin affects many people, not just the ones who do wrong. By giving in to temptation, David set a bad example for his sons and everyone else.

Ark of the Covenant

The Ark of the Covenant—also called the Ark of God and the Ark of the Lord—went with the Israelites on all of their journeys. Inside were the tablets on which the Ten Commandments were written. At one time, manna and Aaron's wooden staff were inside, too. It was Solomon who finally brought the Ark of the Covenant to Jerusalem.

A model of the Ark of the Covenant. Two golden cherubim rest on the lid.

The Ark was a sacred object, so God gave strict rules about how it was to be looked after. Normally, no one was to touch it, even by accident. For example, when David was moving the Ark to Jerusalem, a man named Uzzah touched it and fell down dead. Today, the location of the Ark is a mystery; it may have been destroyed long ago (Exodus 25:10–22; Joshua 3—6; 1 Samuel 6:21—7:2).

Look out for...

As you read 2 Samuel, look out for...

Decisions. *David has to make many decisions as king. Most are wise, but some are foolish.*

Consequences. *David makes a few very bad choices. Those choices have consequences that David has to live through, especially in his family life.*

Crimes. *Several crimes are recorded in 2 Samuel.*

Kindness. *Despite his mistakes, David shows great kindness to several people—far more than people expect.*

Study Questions

- What special promise did God make to David? (7:8–17)
- How did the prophet Nathan draw David's attention to his sin with Bathsheba? (12:1–7)
- How did God punish David for his sin? (12:13–18)
- What sort of men followed King David? (23:8–23)

1 KINGS

The kingdom that David ruled continued to prosper under the rule of his son Solomon. God said he would receive wisdom—and riches and power, too. God allowed Solomon to build the beautiful Temple in Jerusalem.

People journeyed great distances to Jerusalem to hear the wise sayings of Solomon. Solomon, however, married many foreign women, and they each had pagan idols that they worshiped. They turned Solomon's heart away from God.

The rest of this book tells how the nation of Israel was divided into two kingdoms. These were Israel (made up of the ten northern tribes) and Judah (the two southern tribes, Judah and Benjamin).

The people kept turning from God to worship idols. Yet, God did not desert His people. He sent His prophet Elijah to show the people that the Lord is the true God. No matter how wicked the people were, God always had someone to point the way back to Him. The first Book of Kings is full of examples of people who disobeyed God—and of those who obeyed Him.

OUTLINE

The rise of Solomon's kingdom (1—10)

David dies in old age. God offers Solomon anything and is pleased when Solomon asks for wisdom rather than riches or power. Solomon builds the Temple and becomes powerful and rich as well as wise.

The kingdom is divided (11—12)

After Solomon dies, the kingdom divides into the Northern Kingdom and the Southern Kingdom.

Kings and prophets (13—22)

King Ahab lives a life of wickedness. Elijah prophesies to God's people.

The prophet Elijah confronts King Ahab of Israel.

King Solomon's Imports

CILICIA Horses

Tribute
• Nineveh
ASSYRIA

Ivory goods from
the East

MEDITERRANEAN
SEA

SYRIA

Timber
boats Tyre • • Damascus

BABYLONIA
• Babylon

R. Tigris

Susa
•

Grain, oil, wine

Joppa •
Jerusalem •
MOAB

ARABIA

R. Euphrates

Chariots
from EGYPT

• Memphis

• Ezion-geber

Copper

PERSIAN
GULF

EGYPT

Monkeys, exotic birds,
gold, ivory, sandalwood,
precious stones,
from OPHIR

RED SEA

Perfumes, gold,
precious stones,
spices from
SHEBA

Solomon also exported
copper, iron, olive oil,
wine, grain, flax, spices,
and honey to the
surrounding nations.

N

Look out for...

As you read 1 Kings, look out for...

Choices. *In 1 Kings, it's easy to see that the choices leaders make affect many people.*

Good kings. *The kingdoms of Israel and Judah prosper under godly kings.*

God's care. *God takes care of His people. In 1 Kings, we see how He looks after both Elijah and Elisha.*

Study Questions

- How did God show He was pleased with the Temple that Solomon built? (8:10–13; 9:1–3)
- What caused the kingdom to be divided? (12:1–24)
- Why was King Ahab one of the worst kings of Israel? (16:29–33)
- How did Elijah prove that the Lord is the true God? (18:16–40)

Frequently Asked Questions

Q: Since David had so many sons, how did Solomon become king?
A: Solomon was the one David chose to be king. Bathsheba reminded David that he had promised that her son Solomon would be king. In addition, God chose Solomon and promised to bless him (1:15–31).

Q: What did God tell Solomon in a dream?
A: God told Solomon to ask for whatever he wanted. God was pleased that Solomon asked for wisdom.

Q: How did God care for Elijah during the three-year drought in Israel?
A: He sent ravens to bring him food beside a brook and then sent him to the widow of Zeraphath, who cared for him.

Solomon's Temple

King Solomon's Temple was built with the help of skilled craftsmen from Phoenicia. Like the Tabernacle, it had a larger room at the front, the Holy Place, and a smaller room behind that was cubic in shape, the Holy of Holies. The Temple was constructed in dressed stone, with cedar and cypress wood panels inside, large areas of which were covered in gold. In the Holy Place stood the altar of incense, the table of the Presence, and the golden lampstand. Inside the dark Holy of Holies was the Ark of the Covenant. At the door of the Temple stood two huge pillars, named Jachin and Boaz. In the courtyard in front of the Temple stood a huge bronze "sea," used for ritual cleansing, and a massive altar for burnt offerings.

2 KINGS

Relief depicting Sennacherib, King of Assyria 705–681 B.C., on his throne. This mighty ruler tried to capture Jerusalem during the reign of King Hezekiah, but he failed in the attempt.

The second Book of Kings continues the sad story of the divided kingdom of Israel. It tells of twelve kings of the Northern Kingdom (called Israel) and nineteen kings and one queen of the Southern Kingdom (Judah). Most of the kings took the evil path, followed idols, and turned away from God. Only a few were good and tried to lead their people back to God.

The Northern Kingdom lasted only 130 years before Assyria conquered it. Because King Hezekiah and King Josiah obeyed God and the people repented, Judah prospered. God kept Judah safe for another 136 years. However, the evil ways of the people of Judah finally caught up with them. God sent Nebuchadnezzar to take them away into captivity in Babylonia.

During all those years, God sent His prophets to warn the people to return to Him. Most people know about Elijah and Elisha, but as many as thirty other prophets also tried to turn people back to God. God always made sure the people would hear His message, so that they could turn back to Him.

Elijah, the bold prophet of Israel who spoke out against Ahab and Jezebel

OUTLINE

Elijah's final work (1—2)

Elijah is taken into heaven without dying. He passes his power on to Elisha.

Elisha's work (3—13)

Elisha works miracles, including healing Naaman of leprosy. Many kings rule, including Jehu—who kills evil Queen Jezebel and the family of Ahab—and Joash, who repairs the Temple.

Captivity of Israel (14—17)

Israel's kings get worse and worse. They do not obey God Who eventually let Israel be captured by the Assyrians.

Captivity of Judah (18—25)

Hezekiah withstands the Assyrians, and Josiah does away with pagan gods. The Babylonians, however, destroy Jerusalem in 587 B.C. and take many people into exile.

The Kingdom Divides

Frequently Asked Questions

Q: Why did the Israelites worship idols?
A: They wanted to be like other nations and do sinful things allowed by other nations' religions.

Q: Why was the prophet Elijah so special?
A: Elijah was courageous and stood up against evil King Ahab and Queen Jezebel. He challenged the prophets of Baal and showed the people that the Lord is the true God. God showed His special care for Elijah by not allowing him to die, instead taking him straight to heaven in a whirlwind.

Q: What was so good about Hezekiah and Josiah?
A: These two kings of Judah tried to restore worship of the true God. Hezekiah broke down the places of false worship and destroyed idols. Josiah read God's Word to the people and promised to obey it. The people followed his good example.

Leprosy

Leprosy was a serious and contagious skin disease. Anyone who caught it had to leave home, losing his work and family. A man called Naaman was healed of leprosy by washing in the River Jordan (2 Kings 5). Jesus healed people of leprosy more than once.

Old Testament laws taught people how to deal with leprosy. There were certain ways to treat someone with leprosy. It was such a serious condition that when someone with leprosy saw people approaching, he or she had to yell, "Unclean! Unclean!" to warn them not to come near.

Since leprosy was so horrible, it's amazing that Naaman was so reluctant to wash in a river to cure himself. If he had not been so proud, he would have jumped in immediately.

Look out for...

As you read 2 Kings, look out for...

Kingdoms. *A big change is happening in Israel during this time. Kingdoms are shifting and becoming parts of other kingdoms. Kings change often.*

Revivals. *Israel and Judah have times of revival, or returning to God.*

Pride. *Pride is often a problem in Israel. Naaman struggles with pride. The kings of Israel are often so conceited that they feel no need for God's help.*

Study Questions

- What did Elisha want Elijah to do for him? (2:9–13)
- How did Elisha feed his hungry disciples? (4:42-44)
- How did Elisha show that God loves even Israel's enemies? (5:1–16)
- How did King Josiah find the book of the Law? (22:1–20)
- What happened to Jerusalem when the Babylonians captured it? (25:8–10)

1 CHRONICLES

People like to know where they came from and who their ancestors were. The first Book of Chronicles gives long lists of people from Adam to Zerubbabel. It shows how God worked in His people's lives for many generations.

There are lists of kings, members of tribes, Temple musicians, priests, people who returned from exile in Babylonia, and David's mighty men.

The first Book of Chronicles complements 2 Samuel and fills in many of the details. It was written after the Israelites had been exiled. It doesn't deal with all the kings of Israel and their battles. Instead, it shows how David helped set up worship in Israel, taking the Ark to Jerusalem and preparing to build the Temple. Reading 1 Chronicles is a good way to understand the history of worship in Israel and Judah.

King David led the dance of joy when the Ark of the Covenant was brought to the capital city of Israel, Jerusalem.

OUTLINE

Genealogies (1—8)
These lists give the history of each of the families (tribes) of Jacob's ten sons and two grandsons (sons of Joseph).

The generations after the Exile (9)
The Israelites had been captives in Babylonia. Now they return to their homeland.

Reign of David (10—21)
David is king of Israel. He returns the Ark of the Covenant to Jerusalem and wins many battles.

Preparation for the Temple (22—29)
God does not want David to build the Temple, but He lets him gather all the materials and workers together so Solomon can oversee the building later.

Genealogies

The word genealogy is similar to the word generations. Sometimes, instead of calling a list a genealogy, the Bible says, "According to the generations of…." A genealogy is a list of people in a bloodline. It is the history of a family.

The first Book of Chronicles has the major genealogies of the Old Testament. These lists remind us that the people we read about were real people with families.

Look out for…

As you read 1 Chronicles, look out for…

Feelings. *1 Chronicles tells about the emotions of people in the story. David is fearful sometimes. At other times, he is joyful and full of praise. Like us, the people of the Bible have good days and bad days.*

Prayers. *1 Chronicles includes several of David's prayers.*

Lists. *1 Chronicles contains lists of history and descendants (genealogies) as well as lists of warriors and leaders.*

Study Questions

An Israelite warrior

- What lesson did David learn from moving the Ark of God? (13:3–14; 15:1–2)
- What did David say about God's promise to him? (17:16–27)
- How did David help his son Solomon? (22:2–19)

Frequently Asked Questions

Q: What's so important about this book?

A: This book was useful for the people returning to Jerusalem after being exiled in Babylonia. It helped them know how God had worked in their nation. It encouraged them to trust God and obey Him.

Q: Why did David only plan the Temple? Why didn't he build it?

A: David wanted to build the Temple (22:7–8; 28:2–3), but God would not let him. He said David had fought too many battles and killed too many people. God let Solomon, who lived in peace, build the Temple.

2 CHRONICLES

OUTLINE

Solomon's reign (1—9)

Solomon asks for wisdom and builds and dedicates the Temple. The queen of Sheba visits.

Kings of Judah (10—36)

The kingdom divides and Judah is ruled by nineteen kings—and one queen—from Rehoboam to Zedekiah. At God's command, the king of Babylon puts an end to it all.

Though King Solomon was renowned for his wisdom, he later lost his first love for God. High taxes left Israel impoverished and his people angry.

People's lives are filled with many details. 2 Chronicles helps to fill in some facts left out of 1 and 2 Kings. It gives more information about the Southern Kingdom of Judah. It is the second part of Chronicles, as its name says. (1 and 2 Chronicles used to be a single book.)

2 Chronicles was written to show the importance of worship. It tells how the people of Judah turned back to God and practiced their religion sincerely. 2 Chronicles tells the story of Solomon's reign as king. It records how the northern tribes of Israel revolted, led by Jeroboam against Rehoboam, Solomon's son and successor.

It continues to the time when the people of Judah were captured and taken away to Babylonia in 586 B.C. By then, the people had stopped obeying God. He allowed the Babylonians to destroy the beautiful Temple that Solomon had built. 2 Chronicles ends by telling how King Cyrus of Persia allowed the people to return to Judah.

Jerusalem: Solomon's Capital City

Although his father, David, first made Jerusalem capital of the kingdom of Israel, Solomon greatly expanded the city, building himself a splendid palace and constructing the Temple—something God did not allow David to do. The original city of David (left) was joined by fortified walls to Solomon's palace complex and the Temple (far right). In the foreground is the Kidron Valley.

KEY EVENTS
The Exile

1. Judah

Through much of Judah's history, God's people turned their backs on Him. God warned them many times to turn back to Him (Isaiah 2:5–11).

2. Babylonia

Finally, God sent King Nebuchadnezzar to take the people of Judah captive. He destroyed Jerusalem and took the people to Babylonia. They stayed in exile in Babylon until the days of King Cyrus of Persia (36:15–23).

3. Jerusalem

After many years, Cyrus permitted the people of Judah to return to their homeland and to rebuild Jerusalem and the Temple. Zerubbabel led the first group of exiles (Ezra 1:1–8). Years later, Ezra led another group of exiles on the dangerous journey back to their homeland. They rebuilt the walls of Jerusalem and purified the way that the people observed the Law of God (Ezra 7:1–10).

Asherah

Asherah was a goddess of the Phoenicians and Syrians. She was also called Ashtoreth, Astarte, Anath, or the Lady of the Sea. The Israelites began to worship Asherah when they turned to idols.

The second Book of Chronicles mentions Asherah poles, which probably were statues that were supposed to look like this goddess. Whenever Israel turned away from God, they would put up Asherah poles. When Israel turned back to God, they would pull down the Asherah poles (15:16–18).

Frequently Asked Questions

Q: Why did God make Solomon so wise?
A: Solomon asked God to make him wise. He did not ask for riches or fame. That pleased God, so He gave him the wisdom he requested, plus riches and respect.

Q: Just how rich was Solomon?
A: During Solomon's reign, his silver and gold were "as common as stones."

Q: What happened to divide the kingdom?
A: Solomon's son Rehoboam did not listen to the good advice of the older men who had helped Solomon. He listened to young men who said he should be even tougher with the people. That made people very angry. Therefore, the ten tribes of the north followed another king instead of Rehoboam.

Look out for...

As you read 2 Chronicles, look out for...

Wars and invasions. This is a violent time in Israel's history. There is much in 2 Chronicles about soldiers, invaders, and wars. Usually these conflicts come when the nation is turning from God.

Acts of unfaithfulness. Notice how the Israelites change their whole way of living when they turn away from God. Obeying God affects the way we live our lives, too.

Revivals. When a good and righteous king reigns, he leads the people back to the worship of the one true God. Unfortunately, the people fall back into their old ways as soon as a new king begins his reign.

Study Questions

- How did God keep His promise to David? (6:3–11)
- What was Solomon's kingdom like? (9:13–28)
- What did God do when His people turned back to Him? (12:1–8; 33:10–13)
- Why did God punish His people? (36:15–16)

Jerusalem in the Time of King Hezekiah

Jerusalem expanded still further during the reign of King Hezekiah. New walls now surrounded the entire city, which occupied both the Eastern and Western Hill. Hezekiah's new city wall was called the Broad Wall, because it was so wide (21 feet). Hezekiah also reconstructed the Temple and built a huge platform for it to stand on. In addition, he built a new section of the city on the slopes of the Kidron Valley (bottom right).

EZRA

Does God use only people who believe in Him? The Book of Ezra shows how the Lord shapes world events. God had punished His people by sending them into exile in Babylon. When that time was up, God influenced King Cyrus to allow the people to return to Jerusalem.

The Book of Ezra describes two groups of Israelites who returned to their country. The first group was led by Zerubbabel. Those who went are listed by family name. More than 42,000 people returned with this first group. With Cyrus's permission, they began to rebuild the Temple soon after they arrived in Jerusalem. Others gave them silver, gold, and supplies for the task. Not everyone was happy about this. Some tried to discourage the Jews from working. They said God's people were rebellious and corrupt.

A second group went with Ezra eighty years later, during the reign of King Artaxerxes. The Temple had been rebuilt, but the people were not obeying God. For example, they had married people who had idols for gods. Ezra prayed and helped his people repent of their sin.

OUTLINE

Restoration of worship (1—6)

The first exiles return to Jerusalem and begin to rebuild the Temple. Enemies try to stop them, but the Temple is completed anyway.

Ezra's reforms (7—10)

Ezra arrives and urges the people to obey God wholeheartedly. The people listen to him and change the way they are living.

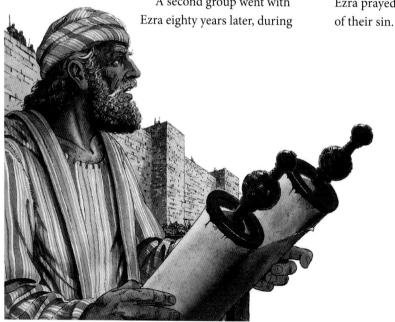

Ezra reads a letter from King Artaxerxes, offering his help in the restoration of the Temple in Jerusalem.

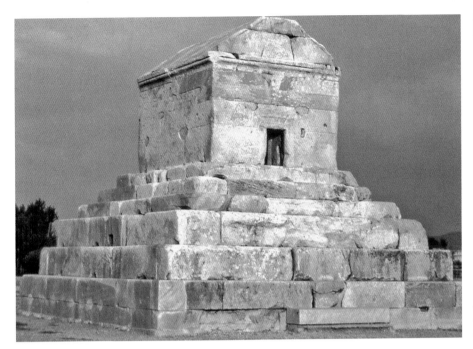

The tomb of Cyrus the Great (559–530 B.C.), founder of the Persian Empire, at Pasargadae, Iran

Frequently Asked Questions

Q: Who was Ezra?

A: Ezra was a priest and a scribe. He may be the writer of most of 1 and 2 Chronicles, Ezra, Nehemiah, and Psalm 119. He loved God and wanted His people to obey Him. He worked hard to help them understand and obey God's Word.

Q: Why did some of the older people cry when the foundation of the Temple was laid?

A: The older people had seen the glory of Solomon's Temple, and they knew this one would not be as beautiful.

Q: Why didn't Ezra want to ask the king for protection for the trip back to Jerusalem?

A: Ezra had told King Artaxerxes that the Lord takes care of those who trust Him. So Ezra prayed for God's protection instead of the king's.

Intermarriage

One of the biggest problems the Jews faced at this time was marrying people who did not love God. God told them not to do this.

The nations around Israel followed false gods. When a Jew married someone who loved idols, the person tended to worship those idols instead of the one true God. This was something God would not tolerate.

Ezra confronted many priests who had married pagan wives. He listed them all. It took three months to sort out everything. Of all those men, only two refused to obey God (Chapter 10).

The Exiles Return

- Carchemish
- Nineveh

ASSYRIA

SYRIA

R. Tigris

Tadmor

Damascus •

• Babylon
• Susa

BABYLONIA

Jerusalem •

JUDAH

ARABIA

R. Euphrates

N

PERSIAN GULF

| 0 | 250 | 500 km |
| 0 | 100 | 200 miles |

- - - - - - *Route of the exiles*

Relief of a Persian chariot

Study Questions

- How did God use King Cyrus to help the Jewish exiles? (1:2–11)
- What problems did the Jews face while they were rebuilding the Temple? (4:1–5)

Look out for...

As you read Ezra, look out for...

Exiles. *In Ezra, the Israelite exiles have been captives in Persia (old Babylonia). They return to Israel in groups.*

Lists. *Ezra gives several lists: lists of supplies, lists of people returning home, and lists of people caught in sin.*

Proclamations. *Ezra gives us the exact words of several kings. They sent out official documents and had them proclaimed aloud to the people to whom they were addressed. There are messages from three kings: Cyrus, Darius, and Artaxerxes.*

NEHEMIAH

Prayer and action are the key words for the Book of Nehemiah. Nehemiah was an Israelite living in exile in Persia (old Babylonia). He was the cup-bearer to King Artaxerxes. This was an important job. Nehemiah heard that the walls of Jerusalem were still broken down after many years. The news made him very sad. He wept and prayed to God. Then he bravely asked Artaxerxes if he could go to Jerusalem and rebuild the walls.

This book shows how Nehemiah prayed, planned, and worked hard. He encouraged the people living in Jerusalem. They needed a strong leader to help them do the work. Enemies did not want the walls to be rebuilt and Nehemiah had to post guards. Many of his men worked with one hand while holding a weapon in the other. Some men even tried to frighten Nehemiah, but he continued to trust God and move forward with the work.

This book tells of the work Nehemiah and the people did. It also tells about their love for God and how Ezra and Nehemiah worked together. Ezra read the book of the Law to the people and helped them learn how God wanted them to live.

The Book of Nehemiah tells how the walls of Jerusalem were rebuilt and how the people returned to God.

Nehemiah oversaw the rebuilding of the walls of Jerusalem.

Nehemiah grew up as a Jewish exile in Babylon and became cup-bearer to King Artaxerxes of Persia. He led a group of exiles back to Jerusalem to rebuild the ruined city.

Persian palace guards, pictured on glazed bricks from the royal palace of Susa

OUTLINE

Nehemiah returns to Jerusalem (1—2)
Nehemiah hears that the walls of Jerusalem are broken. He returns to the city and inspects them.

Rebuilding the walls (3—7)
The work begins, with enemies trying to stand in the way. The walls are rebuilt in just fifty-two days.

Revival (8—10)
Ezra reads the book of the Law, and the people repent.

Lists and genealogies (11:1—12:26)
The people return to Jerusalem and their homes, organized by family.

Dedication and reform (12:27—13:31)
The people dedicate the walls, and Nehemiah begins to change the way they do certain things.

Frequently Asked Questions

Q: Why was a cup-bearer important?
A: The cup-bearer was a trusted attendant of the king. He tasted the king's wine first to make sure it was good —and not poisoned. Then he gave it to the king.

Q: Why were the walls of Jerusalem still not rebuilt?
A: People who were not Israelites settled in the land of Judah when the Israelites were taken captive. Those people did not want the Jews (Israelites) to rebuild their city.

Q: What did the Jews do when Nehemiah wanted to rebuild the walls?
A: They were glad to have a leader. They buckled down and started work immediately.

Q: Why did the people cry when the Law of God was read aloud?
A: They realized they had not lived its requirements fully for many years.

Feast of Booths

Reading the Scriptures, Ezra realized that the people were supposed to hold a celebration called the Feast of Booths. This feast involved making a Booth or Tabernacle to live in for seven days. Ezra and the people were excited about obeying God, and they went out immediately to collect branches and leaves to make their shelters (8:13–18).

The Feast of Booths (also called Tabernacles) was the last sacred feast of the year. It began five days after the Day of Atonement (Leviticus 23:34) and lasted seven days. This feast had two purposes. First, it celebrated the end of the harvest. Second, it reminded the people of the Exodus, a time when their ancestors had to live in tents.

Look out for...

As you read Nehemiah, look out for...

Confessions. *When the people read the Law, they are reminded of their sin. They then confess their sins to God so they can ask Him to forgive them.*

Obstacles. *The Book of Nehemiah is a story about overcoming obstacles. Nehemiah has a long journey to make. People try to stop the building of the walls. Some of the people have disagreements. Some of the Jews have much sin in their lives.*

Details. *Nehemiah has many small but important things to take care of, so he has to be very organized. In fact, this book is a great example of organization.*

Study Questions

- How did Nehemiah answer Sanballat and Tobiah when they mocked him? (2:19–20)
- What did Nehemiah and the other Jews do when they were threatened? (Chapter 4)
- How did the people respond to Ezra's reading of God's Word? (8:1–12)

TOBIT

The Book of Tobit is a parable written around the 2nd century B.C. Originally thought to have been written in Greek (which is why it is not contained in the Jewish or Protestant canon), fragments of an Aramaic and/or Hebrew original have now been unearthed.

The story speaks of God's protection of the righteous, revolving around the travails of two related families: that of Tobit and that of Sarah.

Tobit and his family were exiled to Nineveh where he lived a righteous existence, even when doing so placed his life is jeopardy. In spite of his goodness, he suffered the calamity of blindness. He therefore sent his son, Tobiah, to Media to collect a debt. Tobiah is accompanied by Raphael the archangel (although Raphael does not reveal his true identity until near the end of the story).

In Media, Tobiah encounters and marries Sarah, a woman who had been tormented by a demon who killed seven of her husbands. God protects them, heals Tobit of his blindness, and the family lives a long blessed life in their exile.

The book contains many lessons of living a life of witness to one's faith, especially in one's own family life. It also speaks of the powerful nature of intercessory prayer.

Shalmaneser III was ruler of Assyria at the time Tobit was exiled to Nineveh.

OUTLINE

Tobit in Nineveh (1:1—3:6)
Tobit, an exile in Nineveh, lives an exemplary life, but, nevertheless, is struck with calamity when he loses his sight.

The travails of Sarah (3:7–17)
Sarah, a distant relative, calls out to the Lord in her misery for she had been widowed seven times on her wedding night.

The journey of Tobiah and Raphael (4:1—11:6)
Tobit sends his son, Tobiah, to collect a debt owed him. Raphael the archangel accompanies Tobiah to his destination where he meets and marries Sarah.

Conclusion (11:7—14:15)
Tobiah returns home safely and restores the sight of his father. Tobit and his family praise the Lord for His goodness to them.

Look out for...

As you read Tobit, look out for...

Love so great. *Tobit is willing to place his life in danger to do what was right.*

The power of prayer. *God listens to and responds to the prayers of Tobit and Sarah.*

Everyday holiness. *Tobit gives everyday instructions to Tobiah on how to be a good son.*

Frequently Asked Questions

Q: Why did God not answer the prayers of Tobit and Sarah Himself?
A: God often uses natural means and people or angels to be His collaborators in His works of mercy.

Q: Why did Tobiah not notice that Raphael was an archangel?
A: Angels are technically messengers of God. They sometimes appear in very human form. One could even say that God, at times, uses people to communicate His messages to us.

Study Questions

- Why would Tobit's wife berate him for his good deeds? (2:14)
- What was the attitude of Sarah's parents toward her upcoming marriage? (7:9–17)

Tobiah struggles with the fish that supplies the cure for Tobit's blindness.

JUDITH

The Book of Judith was probably written in Greek (although there are some Hebrew versions); hence, it is considered to be a Deuterocanonical Book, one that is not part of the Jewish or Protestant canon. It is one of a series of stories in the Old Testament (Deborah and Jael, Esther, etc.) in which God saves His people through the mediation of a woman. It was probably written sometime around the 2nd or 1st century B.C.

The first half of the book speaks of the conquests of Nebuchadnezzar (who is said to be Assyrian, even though he was Babylonian—one of many historic inaccuracies in this story) and his general, Holofernes. They are seen to be an unstoppable force. By the end of chapter 7, we see the focus of attention shift to one mountainside village named Bethulia where Judith lives.

A Babylonian warrior carrying a spear

She offers her assistance to the elders of the Jews and then beseeches the assistance of the Lord in her all-but-impossible task. She enters the camp of the Assyrians and wins the trust of her enemies with the promise to give them vital information. She then shares an evening meal with Holofernes who drinks until he passes out. Judith then takes his sword and cuts off his head. The Assyrians flee in panic, and all of Israel is saved through her courageous intervention.

OUTLINE

Israel attacked by Assyria, led by Holofernes (1:1—7:32)

Holofernes, one of the most successful Assyrian generals, attacks Israel and lays siege to the mountain fortress of Bethulia. The leaders of the Jews are unsure how to respond to this attack.

Judith relies upon God (8:1—9:14)

Judith, a widow, encourages the elders to resist the Assyrians in order to protect the rest of Judea, and she places her hopes in the Lord.

Judith defeats the enemy of Israel (10:1—16:25)

Through stealth, Judith kills Holofernes, and the enemy's camp is attacked and sacked. Judith leads Israel in a song of thanksgiving to God Who had granted them victory over their enemies.

Look out for...

As you read Judith, look out for...

Jerusalem. *Jerusalem and the Temple are important for the people of Israel.*

A valiant woman. *Judith is courageous in confronting the elders of Bethulia.*

Not to us, O Lord. *Judith is humble in attributing her victory to the Lord.*

Sculpture of Judith and Holofernes from Florence, Italy

Frequently Asked Question

Q: Why does God act through such violent means in the Old Testament?
A: Many of the stories that speak of God's violent intervention in the Old Testament are more parables than historic stories. Others are episodes in which the people interpreted God's message with their own way of seeing things. This is why we needed Jesus to tell us what God truly wants of us.

Study Questions

- Why do the people fast when they seek God's assistance? (4:13)
- Why do the people not trust in God after all the miracles He had performed on their behalf? (7:24-25)
- What is the significance of saying that God defeated Israel's enemies through the hand of a woman? (16: 5)

ESTHER

The Book of Esther is one of only three books in the Bible named after a woman (the others are Ruth and Judith). It tells the story of a young Jewish woman who becomes a queen of Persia. This unusual event was part of God's plan to save the Jewish people in the kingdom of Xerxes (also known as Ahasuerus).

Haman, the prime minister, hated Jews, and especially a man called Mordecai. Haman plotted to have them all killed. He did not know that Queen Esther was Jewish. Mordecai was Esther's cousin. He told Esther about the plot and asked her to help her people.

Although she was queen, Esther could not do whatever she wanted. No one, not even a queen, could speak to the king unless he gave the invitation. Esther told Mordecai to gather all the Jews in the city to fast and pray for her. Then she would approach the king.

Esther needed great courage and wisdom to find a way to speak to the king and turn the evil plot back on Haman. God helped Esther, and her people were saved. It's an amazing story of God working through His people.

Esther grew up in Susa, the capital of Persia, and was chosen as queen by King Xerxes.

OUTLINE

Queen Vashti is dethroned (1)

Because the queen refuses to appear at the king's party, she loses her position as queen.

Esther becomes queen (2)

Esther's cousin Mordecai enters her in the contest for a queen to replace Vashti. Esther, like other women vying for the king's favor, undergoes treatments; she then wins the king's heart and becomes his wife. She does not tell him she is a Jew because the Jews are captives.

Haman's plans are overturned (3—7)

Haman starts to resent Mordecai, because Mordecai does not show him enough respect. Haman plans to do away with Mordecai and get rid of all the Jews. Esther is one step ahead of him and asks the king to protect her people. The king has a falling out with Haman, who is executed.

The Jews celebrate their deliverance (8—9)

Esther tells the people to celebrate the feast of Purim to remember God's deliverance.

Mordecai is promoted (10)

The king realizes what a useful man Mordecai is and gives him an important position in the kingdom.

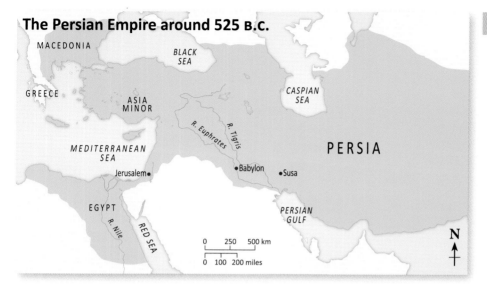

The Persian Empire around 525 B.C.

MACEDONIA

BLACK SEA

GREECE

ASIA MINOR

CASPIAN SEA

R. Euphrates

R. Tigris

MEDITERRANEAN SEA

PERSIA

Jerusalem•

•Babylon

•Susa

EGYPT

R. Nile

RED SEA

PERSIAN GULF

0   250   500 km

0   100   200 miles

N

Frequently Asked Questions

Q: How did Esther become queen?

A: The king wanted a new queen. He had all the beautiful young women come to his palace. Esther won his love and he chose her as his queen.

Q: Why did no one know Esther was Jewish?

A: Mordecai told Esther not to talk about her race or her background.

Q: Why did Haman hate Mordecai?

A: Haman was descended from the royal line of the Amalekites, old enemies of the Jews. Mordecai refused to bow down to Haman.

Q: Why was it so significant for Esther to talk to the king?

A: The law said that no one could approach the king unless the king invited that person to do so. Anyone who disobeyed this law and came uninvited was put to death. Only if the king held out his golden rod would the person be spared.

Look out for...

As you read Esther, look out for...

Opportunities. Esther, Mordecai, and Haman all have opportunities to do something—some good and some bad. Watch for what they do with their opportunities.

Deceit and pride. Many of Haman's actions come from his pride and deceit.

Social customs. Many social customs of the Persians are found in this book. For example, the beauty contest for queen, the way people are able to talk to the king, dinner arrangements, and the feasts all tell something about the people of that time and place.

Study Questions

- What did Haman do when he found out Mordecai was a Jew? (3:5–14)
- What happened to Haman when the king understood his plot? (7:9–10)

1 and 2 Maccabees are two historic books that speak about the time of persecution that Israel suffered during the days of Antiochus Epiphanes, the emperor of the Seleucid (Syrian) empire. The two books were written in Greek and are thus considered to be Deuterocanonical (not contained in the canons of the Hebrew and Protestant Bibles).

The two books overlap. 1 Maccabees covers the period from the beginning of the reign of Antiochus Epiphanes in 175 B.C. until the beginning of the reign of John Hyrcanus I in 134 B.C. Its text is historically consecutive (one event following another). 2 Maccabees covers the period from the reigns of the High Priest Onias III and the Seleucid emperor Seleucus IV (180 B.C.) until the defeat of Nicanor's army in 161 B.C.

The Seleucid empire was one of the successor states of the empire of Alexander the Great. It stretched from Asia Minor to the borders of India. It thus contained people of many languages, religions, and cultures. Antiochus IV Epiphanes, whether through a reasoned policy of unification or a megalomaniac desire to be proclaimed a god, ordered that the Hellenistic culture be practiced in all parts of his empire, including Israel.

Bronze statue of Alexander the Great mounted on his famous horse, Bucephalus

This would outlaw Jewish practices such as the dietary laws and circumcision. Sacred texts were destroyed, sacred sites defiled. There were some Jewish collaborators who supported these reforms. They were opposed by a popular movement led by a priest named Mattathias and his sons, who are commonly known as the Maccabees.

By cleverly combining guerilla warfare with a few pitched battles—along with a brilliant policy of selling their loyalty to the highest bidder during times of internal turmoil in the Seleucid empire—the Jewish people in Israel were able to first acquire autonomy and eventually independence.

The family of Mattathias exercised both the offices of high priest and king, something which many fervent Jews considered to be scandalous. This led to a number of reform movements such as the Pharisees and the Essenes.

2 Maccabees in particular tells of heroic stories of the martyrdom of those who refused to collaborate with the Seleucid authorities. Of particular note are the stories of the martyrdom of the elder Eleazar (6:18–31) who preferred to die rather than give bad example to the youths of Israel, and the family of a mother and seven sons who died for their faith in full hope of a reward in the resurrection of the dead.

The desecration of the Temple was a horrific event which is spoken of in many apocalyptic works of this era in terms of the abomination of abominations. The rededication of the Temple is commemorated in the Jewish feast of Chanukah.

OUTLINE (1 Maccabees)

The heritage of Alexander the Great (1:1–9)
An overview of the story of Alexander the Great and his conquests.

The rebellion of the family of Mattathias (1:10—2:70)
Mattathias and his family rebel against the anti-Jewish decrees of Antiochus Epiphanes.

The leadership of Judas Maccabees (4:1—9:22)
Judas Maccabees, a son of Mattathias, leads the rebelling forces to victory, often against impossible odds. He dies a heroic death in the service of his people.

The leadership of Jonathan (9:23—12:54)
Jonathan, Judas' brother, takes over leadership of the forces of Israel. Through warfare and political intrigue, he successfully gains more autonomy for Israel.

The leadership of Simon (13:1—16:24)
Simon, a brother of Jonathan and Judas, succeeds them and becomes both the political and religious leader of Israel, assuming the role of high priest.

OUTLINE (2 Maccabees)

Letters to the Jews in Egypt (1:1—2:18)
A copy of the letters that the Jews in Jerusalem send to their religious confreres in Egypt, inviting them to celebrate the Feast of Dedication, Chanukah, or Hanukkah.

Introduction by the author (2:19–32)
An introduction to this second volume, which overlaps the incidents described in 1 Maccabees.

A time of persecution (3:1—7:42)
The story of the sad history of the relationship between the Seleucid kings and the Jewish people and their high priests (many of whom acted in collaboration with the persecuting powers). This also includes the story of the martyrdom of Eleazar the elder and a mother and her seven sons.

Victories by Judas and the purification of the Temple (8:1—10:8)
Judas Maccabees is able to defeat the enemies of Israel and conquer Jerusalem and the Temple, rededicating it to the Lord (an action commemorated in the Feast of Dedication, Chanukah).

Renewed persecution (10:9—15:46)
The ongoing battles between the forces of Judas and the Seleucid (Syrian) troops. Those who are faithful to the Lord are delivered from their enemies, while those who are treacherous suffer a terrible fate.

An epilogue (15:37–39)
A short conclusion by the author of this account.

Jewish children celebrate the festival of Hanukkah with special candles.

Map of the Empire of Alexander the Great

Alexander the Great's Empire at its greatest extent

Look out for...

As you read 1 and 2 Maccabees, look out for...

International diplomacy. *The alliance between the Romans and the Spartans with the Jewish people.*

The witness of the martyrs. *The mother of the seven martyred brothers shows a great deal of courage.*

A just recompense. *Antiochus Epiphanes suffers a horrible death as punishment for his persecution of the Jews.*

Praying for the dead. *Our prayers and sacrifices serve the needs of those who have died.*

A Hanukkah lampstand, distinctive for having nine candles

Frequently Asked Questions

Q: Why would some of the Jews have collaborated with the Greeks?

A: It is easy to sell out one's values one step at a time. Those who collaborated probably thought that they were just trying to modernize their faith. They wanted to give up what they considered to be old-fashioned and archaic practices. Furthermore, they wanted to profit (financially and in terms of prestige) by selling out. Sometimes this is done by large and dramatic choices, most often it is done little by little.

Q: Why would someone be willing to die as a martyr?

A: The act of dying for one's faith is the ultimate witness to the idea that we are willing to place ourselves in God's hands and trust in His love and mercy. Jesus spoke of dying to oneself in order to live in Him. Some of us will be called to die red martyrdom (actually suffering and dying for the faith). Others will be called to die the martyrdom of everyday life, what St. Thérèse of Lisieux called a martyrdom of pinpricks.

Q: Why do we pray for the intention of those who have died?

A: There is an episode in 2 Maccabees in which we hear about the benefit of prayer and sacrifice for those who have already died. Our prayer and sacrifice are acts of love that help the person at the final judgment to choose the eternal love. We act as cheerleaders to encourage the deceased to surrender to God's eternal mercy.

Alexander the Great

The faith of Israel was often influenced by what was happening in the world around Israel. Among the greatest influences were the conquests of Alexander the Great (356–323 B.C.) He conquered an empire that extended from Greece to India. When he died, his empire was divided among his generals.

One of them, Ptolemy, became the Pharaoh of Egypt and controlled the territory of Palestine. This area passed to the control of the Seleucids (Syria) in 198 B.C. These two empires were culturally Greek, and they imposed that culture upon the many nations that they controlled.

This led to a period of persecution, especially under Antiochus Epiphanes (215–164 B.C.). It was forbidden to circumcise children or keep the Jewish dietary laws.

The Jews, led by Mattathias and his sons (called the Maccabees) rebelled. Their exploits are recorded in the two Books of Maccabees. Much of the tension of this period is also reflected in the Book of Daniel, which, even though its stories are placed in the Babylonian era, was actually written as a book of consolation for those who were being called to martyrdom for their faith.

Alexander the Great burns the magnificent buildings of the Persian city of Persepolis.

Antiochus Epiphanes desecrates the Jewish Temple in Jerusalem by sacrificing an "unclean" pig on the holy altar.

Study Questions

- How did the Jewish people purify the temple? (1 Mc 4:36–59)
- Why would Judas Maccabees go into battle when the odds against him were impossible? (1 Mc 9:7–10)
- Why did Eleazar not pretend to eat pork to save his life? (2 Mc 6:23–28)
- Why was Onias the high priest so respected by the author of this book? (2 Mc 15:12)

JOB

Job had a great fortune, measured by his vast possessions, which included 7,000 sheep and 3,000 camels.

The story of Job raises questions about why humans suffer.

Good people never have problems, right? Wrong. The Book of Job is about a very good man named Job. God described him as "righteous," a man who fears God and "shuns evil." Yet, Job had more trouble in one day than most people have in a lifetime. In fact, Job had so much trouble that no one could comfort him.

God pointed to Job as a good example of being His follower. Satan ("the Accuser"), however, said Job just loved God for what he could get for himself. Not so, said God, and gave Satan permission to test Job.

In one day, Job's ten children were killed, as were his servants, and all his wealth was destroyed or stolen. Satan expected Job to curse God; instead, Job still loved God.

Satan next wanted to test Job by hurting his body. God gave Satan permission to hurt Job, but he was not to kill him. Satan made painful sores appear all over Job's body.

Job was extremely miserable. He could not understand why God was allowing all this to happen to him, but he never cursed God.

Some of Job's friends visited him. At first, they just sat with him and kept him company. Later, they argued with him that all his trouble was caused by his sin. Job, however, had not sinned—and he knew it.

God did not answer Job's questions. He did, however, help Job see that He is in control—even when bad things happen to good people.

OUTLINE

Satan tests Job (1—2)

Satan comes to God and asks permission to test Job.

Job and his friends discuss his suffering (3—31)

Job and three friends talk about his suffering and why it is happening. Most of their answers upset Job instead of comforting him. They think Job has done something wrong to deserve what is happening.

Elihu speaks (32—37)

Elihu continues to defend God's ways and blames Job for not surrendering to God's will.

God speaks (38—41)

God speaks to Job to explain things. He shows Job how wrong his three friends are.

Job's reply and conclusion (42)

Job admits that God's ways are hard to understand, but he still believes God is good. God corrects Job's friends and then gives Job more than he had before.

Frequently Asked Questions

Q: Why did Satan have power to hurt Job?
A: God allowed it. God gave Satan special permission to test Job's faith.

Q: Does Satan cause all suffering?
A: No. People can make good or bad choices. Bad choices can cause trouble for them and others. Also, sometimes God allows or employs hard things to help our faith grow stronger.

Q: Why did Job's friends think he had sinned?
A: They thought that bad things happen only to bad people. Even Job was confused. He knew he had not sinned, so he did not know why he was "being punished."

"'But the Almighty we cannot find; he is unequaled in power and judgment, and in his righteousness he will not violate justice'" (37:23, NCV).

Suffering

To suffer means to have bad things happen to you. People have faced suffering since Adam and Eve were cast out of Eden.

Often people think suffering is a punishment from God for doing wrong. All of Job's friends thought this. Even Jesus' disciples thought this. In fact, no one can know why God allows this or that bad thing to happen, and we should never assume we do know.

Jesus and his disciples met a man who had been blind from birth (John 9:1–3). The disciples immediately asked, "Why did this happen? Did this man sin or did his parents?" Jesus told His disciples that the man's blindness was not a punishment from God at all. It was an opportunity for people to see him healed by God and be amazed at His power and love.

Bad things happen to people. Even though we may want to blame someone, or perhaps ask God why, we

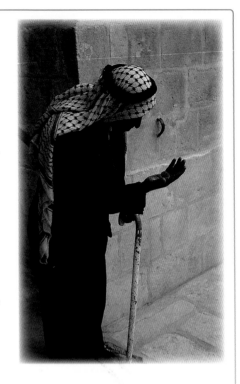

may not get an answer. Whenever we suffer, we should do what Job did. We should humbly admit that God's ways are often beyond our understanding and try to trust in His care and His love.

Study Questions

- What bad advice did Job's wife give him? (2:9)
- What effect did God's words have on Job? (42:1–6)
- How did God feel about Job's friends? (42:7–9)
- What did God do for Job after Job prayed for his friends? (42:10–17)

Look out for...

As you read Job, look out for...

Losses. *Job loses almost everything. Can you think of anything he doesn't lose?*

Arguments. *As Job and his friends talk, they are almost arguing, not because they are angry but because they are trying to make sense of things.*

Job defending himself. *Job is brave enough to stand up to his friends. He has done nothing wrong to deserve such suffering, and he's brave enough to say it.*

PSALMS

Sometimes people don't say what they're really thinking, but the Psalms are not like that—they say things plainly. They have joyful praise to the Lord. They have mournful sorrow for sin. They have prayer for direction and comfort. They have requests to punish people who reject God.

Some Psalms cry out for help in difficult situations. Others ask God for daily needs to be met. There also are prayers for forgiveness.

The Psalms were written by different people. Some are for public worship. Some are private thoughts written when people were discouraged.

There are 150 Psalms. They are attributed to David, Asaph, the sons of Korah, Solomon, Heman, Ethan, Moses, and others. Some have no known author. They teach many things—about God the Creator, His power, and His faithfulness. Many speak of Jesus in the future.

Psalms are actually songs to be sung. The Book of Psalms was the hymnbook of the Jews. Over the years, many Psalms have been put to music for Christians to sing.

St. Paul advises Christians to pray the Psalms, and people in the Church have continued to use them in Mass and outside of Mass from his days until today.

Look out for...

As you read Psalms, look out for...

Instruments. *The Psalms mention many musical instruments, such as lyres and tambourines. Some of the instruments you read about in the Book of Psalms are still in use today.*

Composers. *Many Psalms name their writer. You will see different names, but many are by King David.*

Praise. *A great theme of the Psalms is praise. Songs or Psalms help us praise God joyfully for our lives and all good things.*

An Israelite musician plays on his lyre.

A shepherd in Israel looks after his flock.

Frequently Asked Questions

Q: If the Psalms are songs, why don't they rhyme?

A: Hebrew poetry is different from English poetry; it doesn't rhyme. Instead, the second line often repeats the first line using different words. In fact, almost all Hebrew poetry uses two lines to make its point. The first line says something, and then the second line says it again in a different way. Sometimes, each line begins with the next letter of the alphabet.

Q: Why did David pray to God to punish his enemies?

A: David and the other writers of the Psalms were people just like us; they told God exactly how they felt. They also knew that God is in control, so they asked Him to change things. That's how we should pray as well.

Psalm 23

The LORD is my shepherd;
*   there is nothing I shall lack.*
He makes me lie down in green
*   pastures;*
*   he leads me to tranquil streams.*
He restores my soul,
*   guiding me in paths of*
*   righteousness*
*   so that his name may be glorified.*
Even though I wander
*   through the valley of the shadow of*
*   death,*
I will fear no evil,
*   for you are at my side,*
with your rod and your staff,
*   that comfort me.*

You spread a table for me
*   in the presence of my enemies.*
You anoint my head with oil;
*   my cup overflows.*
Only goodness and kindness will
*   follow me*
*   all the days of my life.*
and I will dwell in the house of the
*   LORD*
*   forever and ever.*   NCV

Musical instruments

Replica musical instruments of Bible times

Many musical instruments are listed in the Psalms. You'll recognize some, such as bells and cymbals and flutes. Although some of the names are the same, the instruments have changed.

The Jews used a tambourine in their worship service, but these tambourines did not have the metal pieces along the side that make the jingle noises. They were like small, handheld drums. The harps were smaller than harps today, and they had only ten strings. The trumpets were long ram's horns or metal horns, but they did not have valves to push one's fingers to make different sounds.

There also were instruments with completely different names, although we have something like them. Sistrums were shakers that were held in the hand. A lyre was a small harp; it was played with a plectrum, or a kind of pick.

The people of Israel used many other musical instruments, too. Music has always been an important part of worship.

Study Questions

- How does David describe someone who pleases God? (Psalm 15)
- Which Psalm did Jesus pray while He was on the Cross and why? (Psalm 22)
- What does David say about a person who asks for God's forgiveness? (Psalm 32)
- How does David ask for forgiveness for his sin against God and Uriah the Hittite? (Psalm 50)
- What are some of the ways in which people can praise God? (Psalm 150)

87

PROVERBS

No one wants to be called foolish. The Book of Proverbs can help make people wise; it is a source of wisdom. Most of it was said to be written by Solomon, the wisest king of Israel. Solomon wrote these wise sayings and rules for living—especially for God's people—but God has given them to everyone who wants to know how to live wisely.

The truly wise person wants to know and love God. A wise person learns how to live peacefully with family, friends, and other people.

The Book of Proverbs is written in Hebrew poetry. It is not the kind of poetry that rhymes. Instead, the lines are in couplets, or double lines. The lines are joined with words such as "but" or "and." For example, Proverbs 10:8 says, "A wise man will heed commandments, but a babbling fool will come to grief."

Proverbs covers every subject one can imagine to do with living. It tells us how to use money, and how not to use it. It tells us the difference between foolishness and wisdom. It tells us how to succeed. It tells us what's right and what's wrong. It even tells us what God loves and abhors.

The Proverbs are important for everyone who wants to make good decisions.

"The aims of the righteous are honorable" (12:5, NCV).

OUTLINE

This book is filled with short verses about many different things. Here are the main topics:

Advice for gaining wisdom (1—9)
Also warnings against foolishness.

Instructions on good living (10—16)
Including advice for families.

Advice for increasing wisdom, understanding, and learning (17—24)
Including thirty wise sayings (22:17—24:30).

Instructions and warnings about rejecting the truth (25—29)
A great deal of good sense.

Examples of wonderful, wise, and foolish things (30—31)
Includes a famous passage on the good wife (31:10–31).

Discipline

Proverbs has a good deal to say about discipline. It says that parents should discipline their children, that people should discipline themselves, and that God disciplines us. So what is discipline?

Discipline is not punishment. God disciplines us by doing something in our life that makes us stop and think, so that we can make better choices. We discipline ourselves when we control ourselves, instead of doing whatever we want, whenever we want, no matter whether it's right or wrong.

Proverbs says repeatedly that discipline is a good thing. We should be open to it and appreciate it.

Look out for...

As you read Proverbs, look out for...

Lazy people. Proverbs has much to say about people who are not willing to work.

Wisdom. Proverbs is a book about gaining wisdom and then living by it. Since God made Solomon very wise, it makes sense that much of a book about wisdom was said to be written by him.

Family guidelines. Many verses are about how parents should treat their children and how children should treat their parents.

Frequently Asked Questions

Q: Who else wrote some of the Proverbs besides Solomon?
A: Other people mentioned as authors of Proverbs are Agur and Lemuel.

Q: What made Solomon so wise?
A: When Solomon began to reign as king, God asked him what he wanted. Solomon asked for wisdom, and God answered his prayer.

Q: Was Solomon always wise in his personal life?
A: No. He made many mistakes, especially in worshiping pagan gods at the advice of his foreign wives.

Study Questions

- What is the purpose of the Proverbs? (1:1–6)
- Why is it important to guard your heart? (4:23)
- How did Jesus use the Proverbs? (25:6–7; Luke 14:7–11)

"For the LORD himself is the one who bestows wisdom; from his mouth come forth knowledge and understanding" (2:6, NCV).

ECCLESIASTES

"I had large herds and flocks, far more than any who had preceded me in Jerusalem" (2:7, NCV).

Sometimes people say that experience is the best teacher, but learning from another person's mistakes is even wiser. Qoheleth wrote Ecclesiastes at the end of his life. If we follow his advice, the things he wrote can help us be wise.

Qoheleth realized that God's ways are not our ways. We must do our best to live a good life in often confusing circumstances.

Qoheleth, or "the preacher," said that apart from God, everything is in vain. If a person is very popular but not a good friend, they will be lonely. If someone has a great job but works only for himself or herself, the job has no purpose. Even expensive cars, big houses, fine clothes, sparkling jewels, money to travel, and great knowledge won't make a person happy.

God made people spiritual beings. We need to know God in order for life to have real meaning.

Look out for...

As you read Ecclesiastes, look out for...

"The preacher, the son of David."
Qoheleth is saying he is King Solomon.

Achievements and riches. *Qoheleth is not shy about telling us what he has done and what he has gained.*

Happiness. *Ecclesiastes talks about happiness more than any other book in the Bible. Notice what kinds of things make people happy or unhappy.*

Frequently Asked Questions

Q: What kinds of things did Qoheleth have?
A: Qoheleth was wealthy. He had delicious food, expensive clothes, a large palace, slaves, attendants, horses and chariots, and beautiful gardens. He was very popular. People visited him from other countries to hear his wisdom. He lived in peace and ease. He had many beautiful wives and children.

Q: Why wasn't Qoheleth happy?
A: Qoheleth forgot to stay close to God. Without living for the true God, he couldn't find peace—no matter how many things he amassed.

Study Questions

- Why should people study Qoheleth's wise sayings? (12:9–11)
- What are Qoheleth's final, most important words of advice? (12:13–14)

Meaninglessness

Ecclesiastes speaks a good deal about what is meaningless. (Some Bibles use the word "vanity" or "futile" instead of "meaningless.") All these words mean empty: something that does not have a reason or purpose. Some Bibles use the phrase "chasing after the wind." It is silly to chase the wind because you can never catch it.

Qoheleth looked back on his life and he realized that so much of what he once considered to be important simply was not.

Qoheleth wrote much about this because he wanted his life to matter. That's how we all are. We want our lives to matter. We want to do something important that makes a difference. We don't want to waste our lives. Qoheleth repeatedly reminds us that if we want our lives to matter, we need to build a strong friendship with God and live our lives for Him. Qoheleth also says we need to enjoy this life that God has given us. Then, when we are old, we will not feel as if we have wasted our lives.

Qoheleth

SONG OF SONGS

The Song of Songs is a love song written by King Solomon. (In some Bibles, it's called the "Song of Solomon.") It tells about his love for his wife and of his wife's love for him. It celebrates their love for each other and the way it brought them together. It also shows that love kept them together.

God created the special love that makes a marriage work. In His plan, marriage is very important. It gives people companionship, pleasure, and a safe place to raise a family. This song tells about two people falling in love, marrying, and growing in their love for each other. The words are powerful, because true love is richly meaningful.

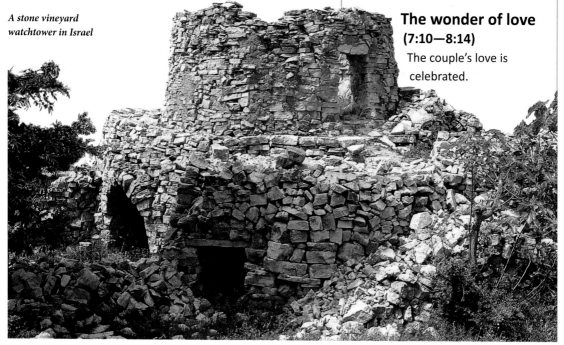

A stone vineyard watchtower in Israel

Look out for...

As you read the Song of Songs, look out for...

Compliments. *When people are in love, they can't say enough good things about each other. That's how this couple is.*

Comparisons. *Often in the Song of Songs the writer compares one thing to another. He says, "She is as fair as the moon." She says, "His eyes are like doves." They find wonderful things around them and compare these wonderful things to the person each loves.*

A bride in traditional headdress

Gazelle

A gazelle, or roe, is similar to an antelope or a deer. It runs fast and can live well in the desert. It is sure-footed and can make its way quickly over rough ground.

The gazelle is also a beautiful animal. It moves with grace and elegance. That's why it's used to describe beauty in the Song of Songs.

Frequently Asked Question

Q: Why is this book in the Bible?
A: It shows how important it is for husbands and wives to love each other. It also shows that marriage is ordained by God. It often has also been interpreted as speaking about the love God has for His people.

Study Questions

- What's so special about love? (8:6–7)
- What advice about love did Solomon's wife have for her friends? (2:7; 3:5; 8:4)

WISDOM

The Book of Wisdom, attributed to Solomon, was actually written very late in the Old Testament period, sometime around the beginning of the 1st century B.C. It was written in Greek (and thus is not contained in the Hebrew or Protestant canon) and shows traces of neo-Platonic philosophy, which was common in that era.

In it, Wisdom is personified as a semiautonomous attribute of God. She offers instruction that confers eternal life. She reveals the fate of the just: eternal reward, and the fate of the unjust: God's punishment. She also unveils the secrets of the universe (times and seasons, the nature of living things, the power of the wind, the uses of plants and roots, etc.). In this sense, her revelation is not only of hidden, celestial truths, but also of the true nature of the created universe.

The book describes Solomon's quest for Wisdom, asking for her more than for riches or fame or even long life.

God, through His Wisdom, has guided the history of Israel. Wisdom came to dwell among God's people and protected them from their many enemies.

Wisdom shows the foolishness of worshiping those things that are not God. The book contains a rather sympathetic explanation for the origins of pagan worship, which, while understandable, is nevertheless pointless. God even punishes idolatry

The Pharos (lighthouse) of Alexandria was one of the Seven Wonders of the Ancient World.

OUTLINE

The fate of the righteous and the unjust (1:1—5:23)

Those who choose evil ways are fated for destruction. Those who choose Wisdom will receive blessing and abundant life, so abundant that even if they were to die, they would still be one with the Lord.

King seeking wisdom (6:1—9:18)

Solomon, the wisest of kings, prays for the gift of Wisdom to accompany him in his life and his reign. He praises Wisdom as the most precious of gifts that God can give, a gift God had bestowed upon his people Israel.

Wisdom in the history of Israel (10:1—19:22)

God cares for His people throughout history. This was especially true in the marvels He worked to redeem His people from their slavery in Egypt. The pagans, who relied upon false gods, faced only trials and death, while the people of God were blessed with abundant life.

with the rabbinic maxim: as the sin so the punishment. Because the Egyptians worshiped their gods under the form of animals, many of the plagues visited upon them were animal plagues (flies, gnats, frogs, etc.).

Wisdom in Israel

The oldest understanding of Wisdom in Israel was folk knowledge—simple instructions on how to succeed that were passed down from one generation to the next.

Slowly, however, the Jewish people began to speak of Wisdom as an emanation from God. They shaped their image of Wisdom upon that of an Egyptian goddess who fostered truth, justice, and order. Wisdom was never considered to be a goddess, but was simply a facet of Who God was.

This became especially important in the era in which the Jewish faith was influenced by Greek philosophy. The Greeks spoke of their god as being totally transcendent, having nothing to do with this world. The Jewish people, more and more, spoke of their God in the same manner. They therefore needed to speak of intermediaries who bring our needs to God and God's revelation to us. Some of the terms used were glory, God's name, God's word. One of the most frequently used terms was Wisdom (e.g., Proverbs, Wisdom, and Sirach). She was God's blueprint and companion in the act of creation, and she revealed to God's people what He wanted of them.

King Solomon, the monarch renowned for his wisdom

Look out for...

As you read Wisdom, look out for...

Good vs. evil. *There is antagonism between the just and the unjust.*

The wrong path. *False reasoning can lead to forms of idolatry.*

Moses and Aaron plead with Pharaoh of Egypt to let their people go. This book calls Moses the "holy prophet" who was inspired with Wisdom.

Frequently Asked Questions

Q: What was Wisdom's role in creation?
A: The Book of Wisdom describes Wisdom's role at creation as a type of architect or blueprint by which God created the world. We thus are able to see God's fingerprints by reflecting upon nature.

Q: If Solomon was so wise, why did he build pagan temples?
A: While he received God's gift of Wisdom, he let himself be seduced by the reasoning of the world. One must not only receive Wisdom, one must then choose to live by it.

Study Questions

- Why do the evil oppose the just? (2:12)
- What is the first step toward Wisdom? (6:17)
- What attributes are given to Wisdom? (7:22-26)

SIRACH

This is a Deuterocanonical Book written sometime in the early 2nd century B.C. It is also known as Ecclesiasticus, a title that means "the Church Book" for it has so much information on how to live as a faithful follower of God (information that was shared with new Christians in the early days of the Church). Sirach was a Jewish scholar who wanted to show how Jewish Wisdom was just as valid and insightful as Greek wisdom. He wrote his collection of Wisdom sayings in Hebrew, but until the 19th century, the only version of the book that was extant was the Greek translation done by Sirach's grandson named ben Sirach (sometime after 132 B.C.). Since that time, excavations have uncovered various versions of a Hebrew original text in Cairo, the caves at Qumran, and other sites.

Sirach's instructions are similar to those found in the Book of Proverbs, but they are given a much more extensive treatment. No longer simple single-line sayings, these Wisdom teachings are extensive poems on how one should act in one's family, in society as a whole, with those in power, etc.

Similar to books written in this era, Wisdom is presented as a stately woman who is an emanation of the goodness of God Himself. She was present at the act of creation as a type of blueprint or architect. She pitches her tent to dwell in Israel. (The phrase "pitched a tent" is the same one used in the Gospel of John to describe how Jesus was the Word that became flesh in John 1:14.) She waters the land and provides it with fertility (like the river flowing from the Temple in Ezekiel 47).

Jacob dreamed of a stairway to heaven when he slept in the desert. Sirach 34:6 warns us to take notice only of dreams sent by God.

OUTLINE

Foreword

A hymn to Wisdom (1:1–29)

A praise of Wisdom as a gift from God to introduce a series of Wisdom teachings for the people of Israel.

Moral instructions (2:1–23:27)

A series of instructions on how to live Wisdom in one's everyday life, whether it be in terms of relations within the family, with those around one in society, with one's leaders, etc. It is good to live a life of prudence and humility.

Praise of Wisdom (24:1–31)

Wisdom is presented as the firstborn of creation, serving as an assistant to God in the act of creation. That same Wisdom visited Israel and showered life and fertility down upon the land.

Further instructions (25:1—43-35)

A continuation of Wisdom teachings concerning how to choose a bride, choosing one's friends, assisting the poor, etc. Wisdom also helps one confront the prospect of illness and death in a godly manner.

Heroes of the faith (44:1—50:29)

An overview of the heroes of faith in Israel to show that their heroes are just as good as the Greek heroes of antiquity.

A hymn of gratitude (51:1–30)

The Lord is a refuge for the one who calls upon His assistance. He is the One Who bestows the gift of Wisdom upon those who seek her.

Look out for...

As you read Sirach, look out for...

Prudence in speech. Caution is to be used when speaking of others.

Faith in the family. Advice on raising children is given.

Moderation. There is the need for temperance in what we do.

The witness of the world around us. We can see God's handiwork in all of creation.

Study Questions

- Should we believe that God speaks through our dreams? (34:1–12)
- How can the work we do to earn a living be part of God's plan? (38:24–34)
- What is the importance of telling the story of heroes of the faith? (44:1ff)

Deuterocanonical Books

There is a series of books in the Old Testament that were written in Greek. These Books—Baruch, Tobit, Judith, Wisdom, Sirach, and 1 and 2 Maccabees—were not accepted into the Hebrew canon when that was defined at the Council of Jamnia in the late 1st century A.D. Only those books written in Hebrew or Aramaic were considered to be part of that canon.

Given that many of the early Christians spoke Greek as their mother tongue, these books continued to be used by most of the Christian community (although some Fathers of the Church such as Jerome questioned their status). One can even point to the fact that Jesus made allusions to ideas contained in these books.

Protestant reformers made the decision to exclude these books from the canon of their Bible, basing their text solely upon the Hebrew canon. They called these books the apocrypha. Catholics continued to use these books, referring to them as Deuterocanonical (a title that implies that while they are canonical, they achieved that status at a second moment). Recent ecumenical Bibles contain these books, although they are often printed as an addition.

A copy of the Hebrew text of the Book of Sirach was discovered at Qumran, near the Dead Sea.

Frequently Asked Questions

Q: What are some of the ways that we can know God's will?
A: At times, we can know God's will by listening to what He has said through the prophets. Other times, we can meditate upon creation, realizing that God speaks through the things that He has made. Wisdom literature reminds us that we also can know God's will by examining our lives and the lives of those around us, for God also speaks through everyday events.

Q: How can we live a most virtuous life?
A: We are called to be virtuous, but Sirach warns us to practice our virtue in moderation. Overemphasis upon one virtue can lead us to make an idol of one idea or practice at the cost of others. Perfectionism does not lead us to holiness—but rather to the attempt to control our own lives and conversion as opposed to surrendering to the will of God.

ISAIAH

Some people want to know the future. Many, however, go to the wrong place to find out what's going to happen. They go to fortunetellers. That is not what God wanted. Instead, God sent prophets to tell Israel what He wanted from the people and what would happen if they did or did not obey Him.

One of the greatest prophets was Isaiah. His prophecies usually had a dual message. Something would happen shortly after the prophet spoke. Subsequently, a second, fuller event would take place hundreds of years later. Some of those events are still in the future.

Isaiah's prophecies were written down in the Book of Isaiah. Many of the things Isaiah spoke about concerned the coming of the Messiah, Jesus.

The Book of Isaiah is divided into three parts. The first part was a warning to Judah, Israel, and nearby nations. God was going to punish them for their sin. Unfortunately, people did not pay attention to these warnings. The second part of Isaiah, which was written by a different author, is full of words of comfort and consolation: the promise of forgiveness is found in the Messiah. The third part of Isaiah, written by yet another author, discusses the difficulties God's people faced after their return from exile.

The prophet Isaiah preached mainly to Judah.

OUTLINE

God judges Israel and Judah (1—12)
Israel and Judah have become sinful nations.

God judges foreign nations (13—23)
Prophecies against Babylon, Assyria, Philistia, Moab, Damascus, Egypt, and Tyre.

Prophecies of end times (24—35)
Isaiah describes a period of dreadful punishment as well as the future reign of Christ.

History (36—39)
Sennacherib invades. Hezekiah is sick. Isaiah predicts that the Babylonians will invade.

A book of consolation (40—66)
Prophecies of redemption and restoration bring comfort to the Jewish people who are in exile in Babylonia. These chapters are often called Deutero-Isaiah (40—55) and Trito-Isaiah (56—66) and might have been written by others many years after the death of Isaiah.

Frequently Asked Questions

Q: Who was Isaiah?

A: Isaiah was an Israelite prophet, the son of Amoz. Isaiah married a prophetess, and they had two sons. Isaiah was probably brought up in an upper-class home. He preached mainly to Judah. He was a writer and messenger to four kings (not counting Sennacherib, the Assyrian king).

Q: How did Isaiah know he was to be a prophet?

A: Isaiah saw God on His throne in the Temple. When Isaiah saw his sinfulness next to God's holiness, he was afraid; yet, God forgave him. God then asked who would go to the people for Him. Isaiah said he would go.

Q: Why did God want Isaiah to be a prophet?

A: The people were disobeying God, turning to idols, and even sacrificing their children to false gods. God was going to punish His people for their wickedness, but He wanted Isaiah to speak to them so they would return to God and not suffer.

Study Questions

- What was it like for Isaiah to see God? (6:1–8)
- What are some of the best-known prophecies about the Messiah? (7:14; 9:6–7; 53:1–12)

Relief of Sargon II of Assyria (722–705 B.C.), who made war on Israel (see Isaiah 20:1)

Look out for...

As you read Isaiah, look out for...

Descriptions of God. *Isaiah uses many titles and descriptions for God. Each is filled with awe and respect.*

Salvation. *Isaiah explains salvation in many ways, including word pictures. He uses a range of images, such as water and white wool.*

The Messiah. *One of the most famous passages that speaks about the Messiah in the Book of Isaiah is in chapter 53.*

Babylon

Babylon was the capital of a country called Babylonia. The city was located on the Euphrates River. One of Babylon's most famous rulers was Nebuchadnezzar (Nebuchadrezzar II). During his reign, more than fifty temples to false gods stood in the city.

It was probably he who built the famous Hanging Gardens that were one of the Seven Wonders of the Ancient World (bottom right). Other famous features of Babylon include the Ishtar Gate, with its surface of blue glazed tiles, leading to the Processional Way; the great Ziggurat that dominated the city; and the Temple of Marduk. The palace of Nebuchadnezzar is the large wedge-shaped building between the Ziggurat and the Ishtar Gate.

Some of the Israelites taken into exile went to Babylon. Most of the events in the Book of Daniel are said to have taken place there under the reigns of Nebuchadnezzar, Darius, and Cyrus.

Eventually, the Jews were allowed to return to their homeland. After some time, Babylon began to decline. Today, it is an abandoned city, buried under sand in the desert of Iraq. Some parts of it have been dug up, but its glory has vanished.

JEREMIAH

Most people don't want to hear bad news. The prophet Jeremiah, however, had a good deal of bad news to tell his people. They were turning away from the true God and following false gods. God told Jeremiah to warn them that punishment was coming soon.

Jeremiah spoke to ordinary people, false prophets, priests, and kings. Baruch, his secretary, wrote down the words that Jeremiah received from God, but the people wouldn't listen to Jeremiah. One king even burned the scroll on which Jeremiah had written God's message. That only prompted Jeremiah and Baruch to make another one.

On one occasion, God used a branch of almond blossom to remind Jeremiah that what He tells the prophet will actually happen (1:11–12).

The coming punishment was fierce. God told Jeremiah not to marry so that he might dedicate himself to God's work and show the people by his life that the end was at hand.

Jeremiah prophesied for forty years. Very few people listened to him in all that time. In fact, he was rejected by almost everyone.

Jeremiah's prophecies came true, however, just as God had said they would. God had warned that Jerusalem would be destroyed by the Babylonian king. Nebuchadnezzar and his army succeeded in doing just that. Thankfully, God also promised that one day Judah would be restored through the Messiah.

OUTLINE

Although it describes true events, the Book of Jeremiah is not in chronological order.

Prophecies against Judah and Israel (1—20)

Jeremiah describes how God called him and then gives several visions (or "oracles") threatening sinful nations with captivity.

History (21—45)

The decline and fall of Jerusalem.

Prophecies against other nations (46—51)

Prophecies against Egypt, Philistia, Moab, Ammon, Edom, Damascus, Elam, and Babylon.

Exiled to Babylonia (52)

Jerusalem falls and the people are taken away from their homes. This is God's punishment for their worship of idols.

Study Questions

- What did God say are the important things in life? (9:23–24)
- What happened to Jeremiah and his friend Ebed-melech when Nebuchadnezzar captured Jerusalem? (Chapter 39)

Potters

In chapter 18, Jeremiah compares God to a potter and people to clay. Potters in Jerusalem found their own clay and removed any stones from it. They then shaped the clay on a wooden wheel. After the pottery was the right shape, they baked it until it was hard.

If the potter went wrong during the shaping, he would simply smash the pot and shape it again. If the pot broke after it had been baked, the potter would throw the pieces into a potter's field (Matthew 27:7, 10).

Look out for...

As you read Jeremiah, look out for...

Sins. *Jeremiah is saddened by his nation's sin and therefore speaks of it often.*

Jerusalem. *The book has two descriptions of the fall of Jerusalem.*

Forgiveness. *Jeremiah speaks a great deal about sin, but he also says that God forgives us when we repent.*

Frequently Asked Questions

Q: What made Jeremiah so brave?
A: God told Jeremiah He had chosen him for the special task of prophet. He told Jeremiah not to be afraid because He promised to be with him and protect him.

Q: Did anyone listen to Jeremiah in forty years?
A: A few did; for example, Baruch, Jeremiah's scribe, and some palace officials who warned the king not to burn the scroll. Ebed-melech, another official, spoke up for Jeremiah when others wanted to kill him. For the most part, however, the people did not listen to him.

LAMENTATIONS

Assyrian relief, picturing captives being taken into exile

Although his prophecies were true, Jeremiah found no solace in being right. He told the king of Judah and the people that God would punish them for their sins. God did as He said by sending the Babylonians to destroy the city of Jerusalem. They captured the people and took them away to Babylonia.

This was the reason why the Book of Lamentations was written. Lamentations consists of five mournful poems. It tells about all the tragic things that happened to Jerusalem and the people. It describes God's anger at the sin of Judah. The author speaks of his sorrow and tears for his people. He had warned them and wanted them to return to God. They chose not to repent and paid the price.

In the midst of all the sadness, the author wrote that people can have hope in God. The author also assures us that God does not give up on His people. God draws people back to Himself.

OUTLINE

The loneliness of Zion (1)
Jerusalem used to be a beautiful and powerful city, but now it is weak and is captured by another nation.

God's anger against the people of Jerusalem (2)
God has finally punished the Israelites for their wickedness.

The author's grief (3)
The author tells God of his sadness. He then remembers that God is always faithful.

Confession and prayers for mercy (4—5)
The author prays that his people will be restored.

Look out for...

As you read Lamentations, look out for...

Sadness. The author is deeply saddened about the sins of his people.

Prayers. Often the author suddenly starts to pray in the middle of his story of the downfall of Jerusalem.

Consequences. In Lamentations, the people of Israel are suffering the results of their sin.

Frequently Asked Questions

Q: Why didn't the author reprimand the Israelites for their disobedience?
A: The author loved his people and the city of Jerusalem. He loved God as well. He wanted the people to love God and enjoy His blessings. He truly was sorry that they disobeyed God and suffered for it.

Q: Why did the author cry?
A: The author cried because his people suffered terrible things: their homes were ruined; families were broken up; people were killed; others were taken away to a foreign country; the city and the Temple were destroyed. His tears had many causes.

Study Questions

- What was it like for the people when Jerusalem was destroyed? (2:11–12)
- What words of hope did the author have? (3:22–23, 31–33)

Jerusalem

Jerusalem was a walled city. When Lamentations was written, the walls of a city were up to 30-feet thick, so it was no small thing that the walls of Jerusalem were torn down. The present walls extend for 2.5 miles and have an average height of 40 feet.

Gates were built into the walls. Jerusalem has eight gates now, though not all are in use. In Jeremiah's day, the gates were closed at night or in times of danger.

Jerusalem was also the capital of Judah and the home of the Temple built by King Solomon. Jerusalem was where the death, Resurrection, and Ascension of Jesus took place. It was the most important city to the Jews. Thus, when the author of Lamentations wept over Jerusalem, he was weeping for the whole nation.

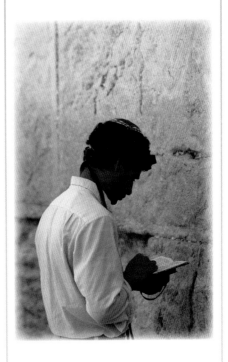

A Jewish young man prays at the Western Wall, Jerusalem, the only part of the Temple that still stands today.

BARUCH

Baruch was the secretary of Jeremiah the prophet, and this book is attributed to him. His name means "blessed." The present oldest text is in Greek (although some believe that there was a Hebrew original). Because it is now found only in Greek, it is considered to be a Deuterocanonical Book and is not part of the Jewish or Protestant canon.

The author speaks of Israel's sinfulness. It has been disobedient to God's command. It therefore fully deserves the punishment of exile that God has brought down upon it. Baruch calls upon the people of Israel to repent of their evil ways and to rely upon the mercy of God, which is great.

There are three main different literary forms in the book. The first part of the book up to 3:8 is written in prose; then, from 3:9 until the end of chapter 5, it is written in poetry. Finally, chapter 6 is written in the form of a letter. It is possible that it was written at different times and was probably

Babylonian spearmen depicted on glazed tiles, ancient Babylon

only compiled in the 2nd or 1st century B.C. (possibly as a book of consolation during the persecution of Jews by the Syrian emperor Antiochus Epiphanes).

Part of the book, 3: 9–15, 32—4:4, is read during the liturgy of the Easter Vigil on Holy Saturday night.

OUTLINE

Introduction (1:1–14)
The Jewish exiles in Babylon send funds to Jerusalem.

Confession of sins (1:15—2:10)
The sufferings that Israel had received were a just punishment for their sins.

Prayer for mercy (2:11—3:8)
A call to God to exercise mercy and compassion upon His people.

Hymn to Wisdom (3:9—4:4)
God has bestowed Wisdom upon Israel, and the greatest expression of that Wisdom is the Law of God.

Encouragement for the people of Israel (4:5—5:9)
If the people do penance, God will turn back His wrath and rescue His people from their plight.

The letter of Jeremiah (6:1–73)
Jeremiah advises the people to avoid the allure of the pagan gods they will encounter in Babylon, for those gods are false gods who have no power to save them.

Look out for...

As you read Baruch, look out for...

The source of Wisdom. *It is important to read the Word of God aloud.*

Mourning and misery. *The extent of the disaster that befell Israel led even to cannibalism.*

Acknowledgment. *There is recognition that Israel deserves its punishment and God is not at fault.*

Belshazzar sees the mysterious writing on the wall, foretelling the destruction of Babylon.

Frequently Asked Question

Q: Is God angry at us when we sin?
A: Probably a better way of stating it is that God is angry for us. As any parent would hate the drugs that were destroying the life of a child, God hates the spiritual poison of sin that destroys us from the inside.

Study Questions

- Why would the Israelites pray for Nebuchadnezzar, the Babylonian emperor who exiled them? (1:11–12)
- What name will God give His people, and what is the meaning of this name? (5:4)

Glazed image of an auroch, ancient Babylon

EZEKIEL

While Jeremiah spoke to the people in Jerusalem, Ezekiel—who was younger than Jeremiah—spoke to the Jews exiled in Babylonia. The Book of Ezekiel tells about Ezekiel's work as a prophet and his message to the exiles.

Ezekiel had been taken captive with King Jehoiachin. God used Ezekiel as an example to show the exiles what would befall them. For example, God told him to lie on his side for 390 days—one day for each year that the Israelites sinned (4:5). Ezekiel delivered God's messages to his people.

Ezekiel said that God was right to punish the Israelites because they were so wicked, yet he also gave them hope. God gave Ezekiel a vision of a valley full of dry bones that became living people. This was a promise that the nation of Israel would be fully restored. God promised to remove their "heart of stone" and give them a "new heart" (36:26).

God once told Ezekiel to build a dirt mound, to represent an enemy attack on Jerusalem, as a warning to the people of Israel.

OUTLINE

Warnings to Israel (1—24)
Ezekiel is called by God to be a prophet. He starts to warn the Jews that God will punish their sin. He prophesies that Babylon will attack Jerusalem. This happens just as he said it would.

Warnings to nations surrounding Israel (25—32)
Ezekiel gives messages to the nations around Israel because they have treated God's people badly.

Visions of the future (33—48)
Ezekiel sees bones coming back to life and begins to prophesy that God's people will be restored.

Look out for...

As you read Ezekiel, look out for...

Prophecy. Ezekiel prophesies about many things that have already come true—and many that are still going to happen.

Repentance. Ezekiel calls on his own people as well as foreigners to repent.

Visions. Ezekiel has several visions that help him understand what God wants to do.

Egypt

The Book of Ezekiel mentions Egypt many times. Egypt was and is a country southwest of Israel. Moses led the people of Israel out of slavery in Egypt.

Egyptian warriors, from an ancient Egyptian wall painting

The famous Nile River in Egypt is so important to that dry, desert country that in the past the people regarded the river as a god. There also are many famous sights in Egypt, such as the great pyramids and the Sphinx.

The Israelites sometimes called Egypt "Mizraim." God's people respected and feared the Egyptians. Several times, Egypt was a place of safety for the people of Israel. When Jacob's son Joseph came to Egypt, he was eventually able to save the lives of his whole family through his work there. Furthermore, when Jesus was born, Joseph took Mary and Jesus to Egypt to escape from King Herod.

One of the huge human-headed bulls that guarded the entrance to the throne room of the royal palace at Nimrud, Assyria

Frequently Asked Questions

Q: Who were some of the other prophets to Israel at this time?

A: Jeremiah, Daniel, and Habakkuk were prophets of God at the same time as Ezekiel. He was not alone. Sometimes it may seem believers are alone, but God always has people who love and obey Him.

Q: Why was God so angry with the Israelites?

A: God's people were behaving as badly as the other peoples around them. They were praying to idols, sacrificing their children to false gods, robbing the poor, and murdering—completely turning their backs on God.

Study Questions

- What is ment by the Day of the LORD? (7:10–27)
- What did God want the people of Israel to do? (18:30–32)

DANIEL

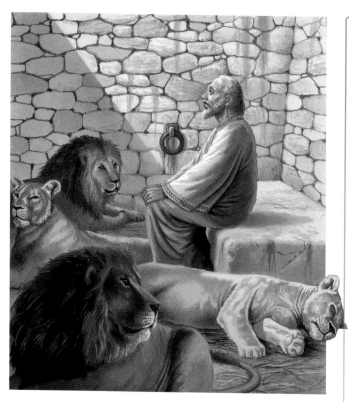

Daniel at peace in the lions' pit

Imagine being captured and taken to a foreign country. Imagine having your name changed and being given strange food to eat. Imagine seeing idols all around and people praying to them. That is what happened to Daniel and his three friends—Shadrach, Meshach, and Abednego.

They all were young nobles from Jerusalem. Nebuchadnezzar wanted them to be trained to serve him. The Book of Daniel records how these young men trusted God even in a strange land.

The Book of Daniel shows how God was in control even when it seemed as if the king of Babylon was controlling things. God gave Daniel wisdom to know what the king had dreamed and how to interpret the dreams. God also helped Shadrach, Meshach, and Abednego to bravely say no when the king demanded that they worship an idol. God performed a miracle and saved them all. The Book of Daniel shows that God controlled all things and had different jobs for each of them.

The second half of the Book of Daniel is filled with prophecies about the future. These also show God's supreme power.

A modern reconstruction of the Ishtar Gate, Babylon, Iraq

A Babylonian warrior

Frequently Asked Questions

Q: Why were Daniel and his friends chosen to be trained for the king?

A: These young noblemen were handsome, intelligent, quick learners, and in excellent health. They were the kind of people the king wanted around him.

Q: Why did Nebuchadnezzar have Daniel and his friends' names changed?

A: Their Hebrew names gave praise to the Lord, while their Babylonian names referred to Babylonian gods. Nebuchadnezzar may have been trying to make them worship the Babylonian gods.

Q: What did Daniel do every day that prompted him to be thrown into the lions' den?

A: Daniel prayed three times every day. The king's officials knew this and tricked the king into making an unchangeable law. The law said that, for thirty days, no one could ask for anything from anyone except the king. Daniel nonetheless continued his daily prayers to God.

Look out for...

As you read Daniel, look out for...

Decisions. *Daniel decides when he is young that he is going to live the kind of life God wants him to live. Each time he makes a decision, it's a decision to follow God's will for him.*

Prophecy. *Daniel explains the king's dreams and tells him about the future. Daniel also describes things that will happen in our future.*

Kings. *The Book of Daniel mentions several different kings. Not all of the information about them is accurate, which leads us to believe that this book was written long after those kings had died, probably around 175 B.C.*

Study Question

- What decree did King Darius make when he saw that God had protected Daniel from the hungry lions? (6:25–27)

Furnace

The furnace that Daniel's friends were thrown into was not meant for people; it was the kind of furnace used for other purposes. At that time, furnaces were used for smelting metals such as copper, tin, iron, and lead. Some also were used for making bricks and pottery. These furnaces were sometimes called kilns. Other kinds of furnaces were used for baking bread. Sometimes the word for furnace was also translated as oven.

The Persians had the idea of using this hot, fiery place for executions. Many furnaces had a hole at the top to throw in materials and a door at the bottom on the side to pull out the metals, bricks, or bread. The fire was especially hot in the furnace the day Daniel's friends were thrown in. Even the guards were burnt to death when they approached it. It truly was a miracle that God protected the men inside the fiery furnace.

Nebuchadnezzar was astonished to see four men unharmed in the flaming furnace after he had three men tied up and thrown into it.

HOSEA

Look out for...

As you read Hosea, look out for...

Meanings of names. Hosea chooses the names of his children for a reason. Notice what these names mean.

Israel and Judah. When Hosea was prophesying, the Jewish kingdom was divided into Judah and Israel. Hosea addressed them together at times and separately at other times.

God's love. The Book of Hosea includes beautiful words of love from God to His people.

The divorce of a husband and wife is a sad occasion. In the Book of Hosea, God compares Israel (the Northern Kingdom) to a wife. He tells Israel that He loves her and wants her to stay; she, however, is interested in other men (that is, other gods).

The prophet Hosea experienced a situation similar to what God faced with Israel. Hosea married a woman named Gomer, but Gomer left him for other men. In fact, other men fathered some of her children. Nonetheless, God told Hosea to bring her home and keep on loving her. Hosea's love for Gomer was like God's love for His people.

The people of Israel were unfaithful to God by putting their trust in military help from Assyria and Egypt. They followed the false god Baal and mixed idol-worship with worship of the Lord. Although they were rich, they were disloyal to God. God sent Hosea to urge the people to return to Him.

Like Ezekiel, Hosea often acted out his prophecies. Here he has a bag of silver and ten bushels of grain (see chapter 3).

115

Jezreel

Jezreel is a city on the border of the land given to the tribe of Issachar. The first son of Hosea and Gomer was named after this city.

The evil king Ahab built his palace in Jezreel (see pages 54-55). It was there that Ahab had a man named Naboth killed so that Ahab could get his vineyard. It was there that Ahab met Elijah and that evil Queen Jezebel met her death. From this city there was an excellent view of a plain called the Valley of Jezreel.

Study Questions

- What did Hosea say when he asked Israel to repent? (14:1–3)
- What did God promise to do if the people repented? (14:4–8)

Frequently Asked Questions

Q: Why did God tell Hosea to marry an unfaithful wife?

A: God wanted His people to see His love as they watched Hosea. The people could see how unfaithful Gomer was and how much Hosea loved her, but they didn't understand that they were as unfaithful to God as Gomer was to Hosea. Hosea and Gomer were an object lesson for God's people.

Q: What kind of things were the people of Israel doing that made God punish them?

A: The people forgot God and His ways. Not only were they turning to idols, but they also were lying, stealing, cursing, murdering, committing adultery, and causing all kinds of violence across the land.

JOEL

Look out for...

As you read Joel, look out for...

Plague. *God often uses extreme natural events to get the attention of His people.*

End times. *Joel describes many things that will happen as we await the end of the world. His language is very apocalyptic and might be intended to be symbolic.*

Study Questions

- What was the army of locusts like? (2:1–11)
- What promise did the Lord give to everyone? (2:32)

How many locusts would it take to block out the sun like a dark rain cloud? That's how many locusts the prophet Joel predicted would attack the crops of Judah. In the Book of Joel, the prophet tried to jolt the people of Judah from their sin.

He told them that God was going to send such a huge plague of locusts that nothing would remain. Every bit of vegetation would be eaten by the insects, and no food would be left.

Some people wonder if Joel was speaking of actual locusts. They think he might have been talking about a mighty army that would destroy everything. Whatever he meant, the destruction would be terrible. Joel urged the Southern Kingdom of Judah to repent and return to God.

Judah was prosperous at the time of Joel. Instead of thanking God, the people turned to idol-worship and sin. They thought everything was just fine.

Joel warned of "the day of the LORD," a time still in the future when God will judge everyone and put everything right. Even though God is the all-powerful judge, He still is merciful. He wants people to repent and turn to Him. He wants to bless those who trust Him.

Joel warns about the coming day of the LORD.

Locusts

Locusts fly in swarms and can destroy large amounts of crops or green plants in a short amount of time. In the Bible, locusts are also referred to as "devourers," "pests," and "katydids." While locusts can eat quite a bit, they also are eaten themselves (Leviticus 11:21–22). John the Baptist ate locusts and wild honey (Mark 1:6).

God used locusts as a punishment once before. When Moses was freeing the Israelites from Egypt, one of the ten plagues was a plague of locusts (Exodus 10:4–15). The prophet Joel describes a terrifying plague of locusts that would come to punish Israel's sin (1:2–4). These descriptions are nothing compared with the prediction in Revelation 9:3–10. The locusts there are described as a great army with the ability to destroy everything in their path.

Frequently Asked Questions

Q: Why did Joel talk about locusts?
A: Locusts travel in swarms and eat all the plants and crops in their path. They can completely wipe out an entire field of crops in hours. Joel said that when God judged, it would be like a storm of locusts. This would scare anyone who knew how destructive a locust swarm could be. God wanted this message to shock the people into listening to Him.

Q: What does it mean to "turn to God"?
A: Turning to God does not mean just going to church or believing that God exists. God wants people to be sorry for their sin and to stop sinning. He wants people to ask His forgiveness. Spending time talking with Him and reading His Word to learn His will is important.

Q: What did Jesus say about the coming of the Kingdom of God and end of the world?
A: Jesus said that the Kingdom was already dawning in His own preaching on life and death. He did not indicate when the end of the world would be; he only gave some signs that would precede it.

AMOS

A farmer speaking to city people might feel worried about telling them about their sin—but not Amos. Amos was a shepherd from the Southern Kingdom. God sent him to warn the Israelites in the Northern Kingdom. The Book of Amos is the record of Amos's message.

Amos began by warning the surrounding nations about their constant wrongdoing. He then spoke against the people of Judah. Perhaps the people of Israel cheered him on, but he then spoke against Israel as well. He said that everyone would have to answer to God.

Amaziah, the chief priest, opposed Amos and reported him to King Jeroboam II. As you might expect, Amos's message was not popular. Amos spoke against the Israelites because of their attitude. They were wealthy and happy. That's all that mattered to them. They neglected the poor, selling them into slavery to buy luxuries for themselves.

The Israelites made a show of religion, but they prayed to idols and didn't follow God. As a result, Amos told them to repent.

About twenty-eight years after Amos finished speaking to Israel, God kept His promise. Wealthy Israelites who sold their countrymen into slavery became slaves themselves. The Assyrians took them away to other lands.

God showed Amos a basket of ripe fruit, warning him: "The time is ripe for my people Israel; I will never again pardon their offenses" (8:1–2, NCV).

Assyrian relief picturing warriors in battle

Frequently Asked Questions

Q: Why did the nations around Israel deserve God's punishment?
A: They had mistreated God's people. Even though the people of Israel and Judah forgot God and sinned against Him, they still were God's chosen people.

Q: What was Amos's message to Israel?
A: Amos reminded the people of Israel about all that God had done to command their attention. God sent disaster and drought, and He sent mildew on their gardens to get them to recognize His power. Instead, they boasted about their wealth and did not trust God.

Q: What sins did the Israelites commit?
A: Their sins were many and varied: they took bribes; they sold the poor into slavery; they pretended to worship God; they boasted about giving offerings to God; they cared more about things than about God or other people.

Plumb line

A plumb line is a cord or a string with a weight tied to the end. Plumb lines were used by masons and builders. They would hang up the string and let the weight at the bottom pull down on it. They would then use the string as a guide, to help them build an upright wall.

The plumb line also was used to inspect a wall to see if it had been well built. This use is described in the vision in 7:7–9. God said that He would hold up a plumb line to Israel. He explained that this plumb line would measure righteousness. It would reveal the sin, which He would then correct.

Look out for...

As you read Amos, look out for...

Messages from God. *More than once Amos says, "Listen to the word of the Lord…."*

Visions. *Amos's visions include fire, a plumb line, ripe fruit, and God at an altar.*

Study Question

• What does God promise Israel? (9:11–15)

OBADIAH

OUTLINE

God judges Edom (verses 1–16)

Through Obadiah's vision, God judges Edom for causing harm to Israel and rejoicing in that harm.

Israel will be restored (verses 17–21)

Obadiah describes a time when Israel will have great power over Edom.

Look out for...

As you read Obadiah, look out for...

Reasons for God's judgment. *Obadiah lists some things for which God holds Edom responsible.*

Signs of Israel's restoration. *God describes the shift in power when Israel secures the upper hand over Edom.*

Brothers should help one other, especially when one is being beaten. The people of Edom, however, did not help their brothers, the Israelites.

The people of Edom were related to the people of Israel because they both had Abraham and Isaac as their ancestors. The Edomites were descendants of Esau, while the Israelites were descended from Esau's brother, Jacob.

The Book of Obadiah tells of God's punishment for the people of Edom because they did not help their Israelite relatives in Judah. When the Babylonians attacked Jerusalem, the Edomites cheered them on. In fact, they actually helped the Babylonians capture the people of Judah. They then plundered Jerusalem and took what had been left behind. The Edomites were proud and thought nothing could hurt them.

Obadiah is the shortest book in the Old Testament, but it provides an important message: God takes care of His people and punishes those who hurt them.

Obadiah warned that the people of Edom were doomed.

The Treasury building in the Edomite city of Petra, in modern Jordan, is cut out of the natural rock face.

Edom

The people of Edom were descended from Esau. Their country was also called Seir, or Mount Seir, situated between the Dead Sea and the Gulf of Aqabah. It was about 87 miles long and 16 miles wide.

When Esau came to this land, he married the daughter of one of the Horites, or cave dwellers, who were already living there. As Esau's descendants grew, they eventually took over the land from the Horites. At one time, King David conquered the Edomites and had control of the whole country. During the reign of later kings, Edom won its independence again.

Esau and his twin brother, Jacob (whose descendants were the Israelites), were often enemies of each other. It is no wonder their descendants mistreated each other and needed God to intervene.

Study Question

• What prophecy did Obadiah make about Israel and Edom? (verses 17–18)

Frequently Asked Questions

Q: Where did the Edomites live?
A: The Edomites lived south of Judah. They shared a boundary with Judah and were close enough to help the people of Judah.

Q: Why were the Edomites so proud?
A: The people of Edom had carved a city out of the rocks. Being very proud of themselves, they lived high up in a fortress that seemed secure, and they thought they were safe.

Q: How did God judge Edom?
A: The nation of Edom was completely destroyed.

JONAH

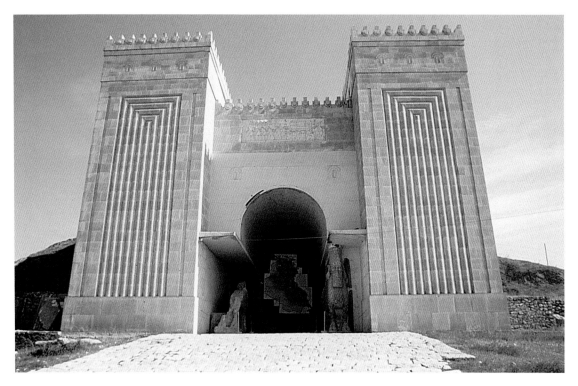

The Hebrew people had a difficult time learning that God wanted them to obey Him. After they had learned that lesson, however, they found it difficult to understand that God still loved people of other nations. The Book of Jonah tells about Jonah's problem understanding that God loves everyone.

This is the only book of prophecy that tells more about the prophet than about the prophet's message.

Jonah was the first Jewish prophet sent on a mission to a non-Jewish country. He was a prophet to the Northern Kingdom of Israel. God then sent him to Nineveh, the capital of the great Assyrian Empire.

The Assyrians were neither friendly nor nice; they were fierce and cruel warriors. When God told Jonah to go to Nineveh to preach to its people, Jonah went off in the opposite direction.

Jonah tried to get as far away as possible. Even being in a ship in the middle of the Mediterranean Sea, Jonah could not hide from God. After suffering for disobeying Him, Jonah repented and obeyed God's instructions.

Jonah preached to the people and they converted. Thus, Jonah learned that God's salvation is for all who repent and believe.

A reconstruction of one of the gates of the ancient city of Nineveh

A Phoenician vessel, possibly similar to the boat Jonah boarded at Joppa to take him across the Mediterranean Sea

OUTLINE

Jonah's call and escape (1)

God asks Jonah to go to Nineveh, but Jonah runs off the opposite way. During a storm, Jonah is thrown overboard from a boat and rescued by a large fish.

Jonah's prayer (2)

Jonah thanks and praises God for saving him, and the fish spits Jonah out onto the shore.

Preaching to Nineveh (3)

Jonah obeys God and preaches to the people of Nineveh.

Jonah is disappointed (4)

The people of Nineveh repent, and Jonah is disappointed that God doesn't punish them for their sins.

Frequently Asked Questions

Q: Why didn't Jonah want to preach to the people of Nineveh?

A: The people of Nineveh were very cruel enemies of Israel and Jonah hated them. Jonah knew that God is merciful and kind, and he didn't want the Ninevites to repent because he also knew God would forgive them if they did. Jonah wanted them to be punished for their wickedness.

Q: How did Jonah get swallowed by a fish?

A: God sent the fish to rescue Jonah from drowning in the sea. In fact, He sent the fish in answer to Jonah's prayer for help. The fish took Jonah to shore from the middle of the sea.

Jonah's Adventures

Carchemish

Nineveh

ASSYRIA

SYRIA

R. Tigris

MEDITERRANEAN
SEA

Tadmor

Damascus

Babylon

Susa

BABYLONIA

Joppa

Jerusalem

JUDAH

ARABIA

Memphis

PERSIAN
GULF

EGYPT

RED SEA

- - - - - *Jonah runs away to sea*
- - - - - *Jonah goes to Nineveh*

0   250   500 km
0   100   200 miles

N

Nineveh

Nineveh was one of the most ancient cities of the world. It was founded on the banks of the River Tigris. For many years it was capital of the Assyrian Empire and was an important city from the time of King David until the reign of Manasseh.

Nineveh was ruled by kings, except for about fifty years around 800 B.C., probably about the time when Jonah went to Nineveh and saw the people there repent of their sin.

Nineveh was destroyed by the Assyrians around 612 B.C., just after Nahum prophesied against the city.

Look out for...

As you read Jonah, look out for...

Jonah's pride. *It shows up more than once.*

Jonah's prayers. *In his prayers, Jonah is honest with God, even when he is angry.*

Study Questions

- What was it like for Jonah in the sea and inside the fish? (2:1–9)
- What happened when Jonah preached to the people of Nineveh? (3:1–10)
- Why did Jonah become angry? (4:1–4)

MICAH

It's not enough for people to worship God but forget what He teaches them. God expects people who love Him to be kind and merciful to others. He wants them to do good. He also wants them to worship Him sincerely.

The prophet Micah explained this in the Book of Micah. He said God would judge Samaria (in Israel) and Jerusalem (in Judah) for disobeying God. He also told them that the Messiah would bring hope and peace.

Hundreds of years before Jesus was born, Micah predicted that the Messiah would be born in Bethlehem. It was this prediction that the wise men followed. They asked King Herod in Jerusalem where the new King was. The priests told them He was in Bethlehem.

Micah was a prophet at the same time as Isaiah and Hosea. His book is written in Hebrew poetry. He condemned those who stole, lied, oppressed the poor, murdered, craved money, and pretended to worship God.

The prophet Micah wrote in poetry rather than prose.

While Micah was a prophet, Assyria overran Israel. Micah predicted that Judah would fall as well. The Messiah would be the new King—a righteous, good King.

OUTLINE

Lying prophets (1—3)
Micah speaks directly to Samaria and Jerusalem (the two Jewish capitals) about the sin of the people and of the leaders.

Christ's coming Kingdom (4—5)
Micah predicts Jesus' birth and never-ending reign.

God judges and forgives (6—7)
Micah sets out both God's case against Israel and Israel's hope of God's forgiveness.

Look out for...

As you read Micah, look out for...

The Messiah. *Micah tells about Jesus' coming long before it happens. He even names the town where Jesus will be born.*

Advice. *Micah gives good advice on how to follow God in our everyday lives.*

Samaria. *Micah talks a great deal about the punishment the people of Samaria will receive for their sins.*

Samaria

Samaria can mean a city, a region, or a country. When the Israelite kingdom split into the Northern and Southern Kingdoms, the Northern Kingdom built the city of Samaria as its capital. The land where they built the city was bought from a man named Shemer, and it's from this word that the city got its name.

The Northern Kingdom was made up of ten tribes of Israelites. Sometimes people refer to Samaria as all the land held by those ten tribes.

Micah prophesied to both the city of Samaria (capital of the Northern Kingdom) and the city of Jerusalem (capital of the Southern Kingdom). Both cities were full of Israelites who had disobeyed and forgotten the one true God.

Samaria was built on a hill. It had a wall all the way around it (like most cities at that time) and gates that could be closed at night and during an attack. Samaria stood through many battles, and its ruins still exist today.

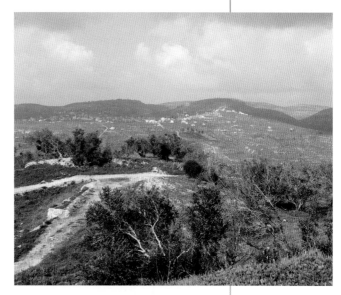

A view of the site of the city of Samaria today

Frequently Asked Questions

Q: Why would God punish Israel and Judah?
A: The people were ignoring God's instructions to treat each other with respect. They were taking property from widows and other poor people. False prophets were saying everything was fine. God wanted them to know that these matters were important.

Q: If God loves His people, how could He hurt them?
A: It is precisely because God loves people that He punishes sin. He wants people to repent and turn to Him. Sometimes when people are enjoying God's blessings, they forget Him. He takes action to get their attention. In some instances, He does that by punishing them.

Q: How were the priests pretending to worship God?
A: The priests carried out the correct ceremonies, but in their hearts they were scheming to get money and power.

Study Questions

• What prophecy of Micah came true in Bethlehem? (5:2–5; Matthew 2:1–6)
• How does Micah describe God? (7:18–20)

NAHUM

An Assyrian army attacks an Israelite city. Assyrian soldiers were greatly feared in the ancient world. They captured many towns and cities of Israel and Judah.

An Assyrian warrior

Some nations are so powerful that it seems as if they can never be defeated. That was the case with Assyria, which had a huge, powerful, fierce army.

The Assyrians had strong chariots with sharp knives sticking out of their wheel hubs. The soldiers were not afraid of anyone. They therefore killed more people than could be counted and plundered nation after nation. Since they had no sense of right and wrong, being cruel to their prisoners had no effect on them.

Nahum was a prophet in the 7th century B.C., and he hated the wicked and brutal practices of the Assyrians.

Nahum's book is God's message to Nineveh, the great capital of Assyria. The news was not good; God had run out of patience with Nineveh. The Assyrians had taken Israel

OUTLINE

God's nature (1)
God's anger, patience, and power.

Nineveh's destruction (2—3)
Nahum describes the destruction of Nineveh and God's reasons for destroying it.

captive. Now God, the righteous Judge, was going to destroy wicked Assyria. The Assyrians were to feel the full force of God's power.

There is also good news in the Book of Nahum: God promised the people of Judah that Assyria would never again harm them.

Assyria

Assyria was right beside Babylonia. They fought constantly and moved their border back and forth. Israel was next to both of these empires and often had to fight them. Israel was taken over by both empires for a time.

Assyria was probably started by a colony of Babylonians, so their culture and religion were similar. The Assyrians regarded the false god Asshur as their founder. Their other gods included Anu, Bel, Ea, Shamash, and Ishtar. While the Assyrians fought the Babylonians, at times they worked together and almost gained control of the whole region. Assyria's capital was Nineveh.

Assyrian relief depicting an archer and an infantryman

Look out for...

As you read Nahum, look out for...

God's nature. *Even though this is a prophecy against Assyria, this book tells us a great deal about God.*

Punishment. *Nahum makes it clear that the people of Assyria will be punished severely for their sin.*

Study Question

• Why do some people say that God is angry all the time, while others say He is loving? (1:7–8)

Frequently Asked Questions

Q: How did God destroy Assyria?
A: God used other nations to destroy Assyria. In 612 B.C., He used the Babylonians and the Medes to fight Assyria. They did to Assyria what it had done so many times to other nations: they waged war against the people and took all their wealth. The city of Nineveh was so completely destroyed that no one could identify its ruins until 1845—more than 2,000 years later!

Q: How was the city of Nineveh proven to be so weak?
A: Water came flowing down in a rush when the enemy broke the dikes that lay upstream.

HABAKKUK

A mythical creature depicted in glazed tiles from a wall in ancient Babylon

It is difficult to watch or read the news these days. People steal, lie, cheat, attack others, kill their enemies—and their friends—and do many other evil things. It may not be so hard to believe that the news was no different at the time in which the prophet Habakkuk lived in Judah more than 2,500 years ago.

Habakkuk had the same questions that many people have today. He asked God why He wasn't doing anything about all this evil. Habakkuk knew God is just and holy, so he couldn't understand how God could let the evil people get away with doing wicked things.

Habakkuk did the right thing with his questions by going to God with them. God answered him and gave him a message that people can still read today.

God had a plan that was stranger than anything Habakkuk could imagine. God was going to use the Babylonians to punish the people of Judah.

This created more questions for Habakkuk. The Babylonians were far more wicked than the people of Judah. How could God use them to punish His people? The Babylonians were proud. They didn't know that God was using them to turn His people back to Him. The Babylonians' sins would be their undoing.

God assured Habakkuk that one day He would punish all those who are against Him, but those who trust in God will have true life (2:4).

Babylonia

Babylonia was a powerful kingdom known for many things, especially two famous cities. The capital city of Babylonia was Babylon, mentioned in both the New and Old Testaments. Another important Babylonian city was Ur, the place from which Abraham came.

Babylonia is famous for its unique style of pottery, the beginnings of writing called cuneiform, the oldest ziggurat at that time, and a special style of weaving (see Joshua 7:21). Because the country was so large and so close to the Jewish nation, it always was a

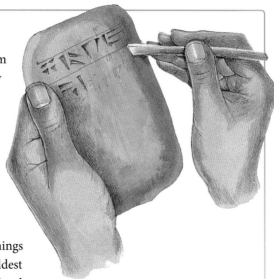

Cuneiform writing was done using a wedge-shaped stylus in damp clay. The clay was later hardened into a tablet to preserve the message.

threat. Countries at that time were forever trying to widen their borders and seize other countries.

Look out for...

As you read Habakkuk, look out for...

Questions. *Habakkuk asks God some hard questions.*

Answers. *God answers Habakkuk's questions.*

Praises. *Habakkuk praises God for His greatness.*

Study Questions

- What promises did God give to Habakkuk? (2:14, 20)
- How did Habakkuk praise God? (3:1–19)
- What did Habakkuk promise God? (3:17–18)

Frequently Asked Questions

Q: What did God do when Habakkuk asked hard questions?
A: God didn't get angry with Habakkuk. He answered his questions and explained that justice would be done. God said there was a set time for this and told Habakkuk to be patient and wait for it.

Q: What did Habakkuk do with God's answers?
A: At first, Habakkuk was even more confused. He then saw that God is in control. He asked God to have mercy on Judah when the time of discipline came, and then he praised God.

ZEPHANIAH

OUTLINE

God will judge Judah soon (1—2:3)

Zephaniah prophesies that soon Jerusalem will be destroyed.

God will judge all nations (2:4–15)

Zephaniah prophesies about the time when God will judge the whole world.

Jerusalem rebels and is redeemed (3)

God will one day purify His people.

Prisoners from Judah are marched into exile by the cruel Babylonians.

Relief of the Canaanite deity Baal

God had sent many prophets to warn the people of Judah that He would judge them soon. The Book of Zephaniah was one of the last written before the Jews were exiled to Babylonia.

Zephaniah prophesied during the reign of King Josiah of Judah. He also prophesied when Jeremiah started giving God's messages to the people of Jerusalem. King Josiah was the last good king of Judah. He worked hard to lead the people away from idols and back to God. It is likely that Zephaniah helped Josiah to understand God's Word and to apply it to his people.

Manasseh and Amon, two kings before Josiah, had led the people far from God. They had turned to idols such as Baal, Molech, and others. Molech-worship included sacrificing children, and this displeased God greatly. The people thought they could worship both the true God and idols.

The "day of the Lord" that Zephaniah predicted had two meanings: first, the Babylonian Exile; second, the last days. At that time, God will punish all who have rejected Him. Those who trust in Him will live with Him in heaven.

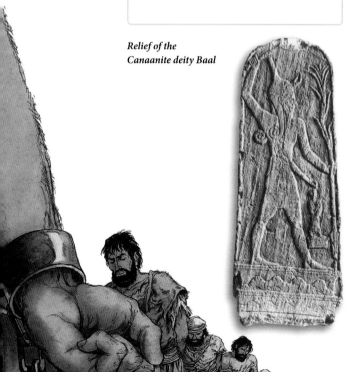

Moab and Ammon

The countries of Moab and Ammon were named after the families or tribes that settled there. The families were named after their most important ancestor.

Lot was Abraham's nephew. He became involved with two very sinful cities, Sodom and Gomorrah. After he left those cities, each of his daughters had a son. The names of these sons were Moab and Ammon. When Moab and Ammon grew up, they moved away, and their families settled in these lands that were then named after them. After many years, the people of Israel (Abraham's descendants) came back to settle their land, and the people of Moab and Ammon fought against them.

Zephaniah prophesied against Moab and Ammon because they fought against Israel, tried to take land that was not theirs, and attempted to persuade Israel to be unfaithful to God.

The barren hills of Moab, with the Dead Sea in the distance

Frequently Asked Questions

Q: If King Josiah and Zephaniah helped the people turn back to God, why did God still punish them?

A: Josiah truly wanted to please God, but most of his people did not have a real change of heart. A few years after King Josiah died, the people continued their sinful ways.

Q: How can Zephaniah's prophecy have two meanings?

A: Actually, several prophecies in the Old Testament have dual meanings. The first meaning came about soon after the prophet had spoken, while the second meaning would manifest itself later. Some of Zephaniah's prophecies tell of events still in the future.

Look out for…

As you read Zephaniah, look out for…

Day of the LORD. Zephaniah talks about two days of the LORD. These are days when God intervenes in the world in a major way. One of those days will be at the end of the world as we know it.

Joy. Even though Zephaniah is talking about punishment, there is a great deal of joy at the end of his message.

Study Question

• What good promise did God make to Israel? (3:14–20)

HAGGAI

Soon after King Cyrus defeated the Babylonians, he let the Jews return to Jerusalem to rebuild the Temple. The returned exiles started this task, but enemies threatened and discouraged them. For as many as ten years, they stopped work on the Temple. God sent the prophet Haggai to prompt the people to finish the job.

Haggai's messages are recorded in the Book of Haggai. Haggai and Zechariah worked with Ezra to help the Jews.

Haggai reminded the Jews that it was important to rebuild God's Temple as well as their own homes.

The Jewish people were busy building their own homes, but left God's Temple in ruins. Haggai said this wasn't right, and he reminded them that they needed to finish the Temple. Although they were working hard, they had little to show for it. Haggai told them that this was because God was working against them.

OUTLINE

Rebuilding the Temple (1:1—2:9)
Haggai encourages the people to rebuild the Temple now and stop delaying.

Promises (2:10–23)
God promises to meet the people's needs if they will finish their work on the Temple.

Haggai said the people should put first things first: they should rebuild God's Temple. They should care about spiritual matters; God then would satisfy their needs and their hearts.

View of the Old City of Jerusalem, Israel, and the Temple Mount from the Mount of Olives

The Temple

Solomon built the first Temple with the finest building materials. Each time the Israelites turned away from God, however, they stopped taking care of it. Furthermore, each time enemies fought them, those enemies would try to destroy it. Therefore, we often read in the Old Testament about the Temple being rebuilt.

During the time of Haggai, the Temple had been completely destroyed. The Israelites did not have much money or many resources to build a beautiful Temple again, but they tried. Zerubbabel was the governor in charge of the city. Joshua (not Moses' successor) was their religious ruler. Together, they led the people to rebuild the Temple. It was not as fine as Solomon's Temple, but it reminded the people that it was important to worship God.

Frequently Asked Questions

Q: What were the people doing in Jerusalem all those years?
A: They settled down to live and to build their own homes, some of which were expensive. They also grew a great deal of grain, grapes, and olive trees, but they weren't rebuilding the Temple.

Q: What did the people do after Haggai spoke to them?
A: The leaders and the people quickly followed Haggai's advice. Within weeks, they proceeded to rebuild the Temple.

Q: After the people obeyed Him, what did God do?
A: As soon as the people started work on the Temple, God said He would bless them and make their crops grow.

Look out for...

As you read Haggai, look out for...

Dates. This book gives us the dates of Haggai's messages.

Inspiration. Haggai encouraged God's people to work on the Temple.

Results. The people responded to Haggai and rebuilt the Temple.

Study Questions

- How did God encourage His people? (2:4–5)
- What did God say to the people as soon as they started work? (2:18–19)

ZECHARIAH

God gave the prophets messages about the future. Some of these messages were warnings that God would judge the people if they didn't repent of sin and turn to Him. Some messages gave hope of comfort and peace.

Zechariah was a prophet who had returned from exile to Jerusalem. He worked with the prophet Haggai to encourage the people to continue rebuilding the Temple. His message told of God's anger and His love.

Of all the Old Testament books, the Book of Zechariah is filled with the most prophecies about the Messiah. There are prophecies about His First Coming to earth and when He was crucified and rose again. There are prophecies about His Second Coming as King. There also are many prophecies about the end of time.

God doesn't give us exact dates, but He warns us not to follow false prophets. He promises that, at the end of time, those who reject God will be punished forever; those who trust Jesus Christ, the Messiah, will enjoy His peace and everlasting life.

OUTLINE

Introduction and visions (1—6)
Zechariah tells about visions of horns, blacksmiths, olive trees, lampstands, and flying scrolls.

True worship (7—8)
Zechariah encourages his people to trust God and to repair the Temple.

The future of Israel (9—14)
Zechariah predicts that God will judge Israel's enemies, protect Israel, and rule the earth.

Like Haggai, the prophet Zechariah urged the people to trust God and rebuild the Temple.

Myrtle trees

In one of Zechariah's visions, he sees a man (who really was an angel) standing among some myrtle trees. A myrtle is a small evergreen shrub with white flowers, blue berries, and scented leaves. The Jews thought that this plant stood for peace and prosperity. When the Jews celebrated their Feast of Booths (or Tabernacles), they used myrtle branches to cover the shelters in which they lived.

Zechariah thought of the myrtle as a plant of peace; therefore, it must have been comforting for Zechariah to receive good news from an angel who was surrounded by myrtles.

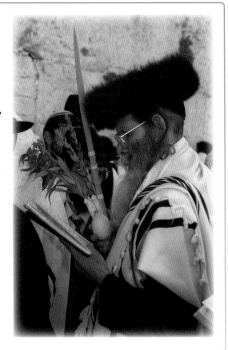

An Orthodox Jew holding myrtle twigs, together with other plants associated with the Feast of Booths, or Sukkot

Look out for...

As you read Zechariah, look out for...

Visions. *Zechariah has eight visions.*

Prophecies. *Zechariah makes many prophecies that came true in the life of Jesus.*

Study Questions

- What instructions did God give the people? (8:16–17)
- How does Zechariah's prophecy about the king compare with Jesus' enactment of the prophecy? (9:9–10; Matthew 21:1–11)

Frequently Asked Questions

Q: **How do we know that Jesus is the Messiah that Zechariah was talking about?**
A: Zechariah wrote his prophecies about 500 years before Jesus was born, and Jesus' life matches many details given in Zechariah's prophecies. Jesus is the only One who fits the description Zechariah gave.

Q: **What is the significance of Jesus' life matching these prophecies?**
A: Since God's Word is true concerning Jesus' First Coming to earth, we can be confident that His other promises are true as well. God warns that He is going to judge people and promises blessings for those who love Him.

MALACHI

Malachi was the last of the prophets to Judah and Israel. The Temple had been rebuilt, and the walls of Jerusalem had been completed, but the people were deficient in their worship of God.

So much had gone awry: the priests were not offering sacrifices properly; men were divorcing their wives and marrying younger women who prayed to idols; children were growing up believing in idols; and the people weren't tithing their crops and animals to God. This was tantamount to stealing from God.

Malachi made it clear that God's people had to take their worship more seriously and promised blessing for those who did. His very last words told of another prophet who would help the people before God judged them.

As already stated, Malachi was the last of the prophets to Israel and Judah—until John the Baptist proclaimed the coming of Jesus.

OUTLINE

Worthless worship
(1:1—2:9)
God confronts Israel's leaders about their sin.

A call to repent (2:10–17)
Malachi reminds his people to trust God and be faithful to Him.

God will judge people (3–4)
Malachi predicts that God will judge and purify people.

Model of first-century Jerusalem, showing the Temple Mount area (top left)

Grapes

Often in the Old Testament, when a prophet talks about a time when things are going well, he mentions grapes. Sometimes he says that grapes will bring much wine. Sometimes, as in Malachi, he says the grapes won't wither.

Grapes are one of the first plants mentioned in the Bible (Genesis 9:20). They grow on climbing vines that can either be left to grow wild or can be cultivated in vineyards. For the Jews, grapes were a symbol of wealth and good fortune. The grape harvest was a time of celebration and rejoicing.

Look out for...

As you read Malachi, look out for...

Questions and answers. *Malachi uses questions and answers throughout his messages.*

Priests. *Much of what Malachi says about priests encourages church leaders today to reflect on the seriousness of their ministry.*

Study Questions

- How did the people weary God? (2:17)
- Who is the prophet like Elijah whom God promised? (3:1; Matthew 17:10–13)
- How will God treat those who trust Him? (3:16–18)

Frequently Asked Questions

Q: What was wrong with sacrificing a sick animal?
A: God used sacrifices to show the seriousness of sin and the need for forgiveness. God is holy and requires our best—not something sick or broken.

Q: How did the priests worship poorly?
A: The priests weren't showing respect to God, and they complained about making sacrifices. As leaders, they influenced people's attitudes and actions. Furthermore, they weren't teaching the truth.

Q: Why does God not abide divorce?
A: God wants husbands and wives to love each other and be faithful to one another. He knows that people, especially children, are hurt badly when there is a divorce. He wants families to be the source of safety and happiness in which children can grow.

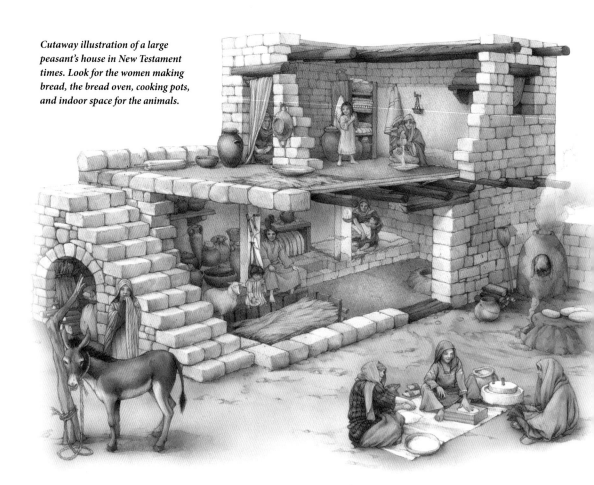

Cutaway illustration of a large peasant's house in New Testament times. Look for the women making bread, the bread oven, cooking pots, and indoor space for the animals.

The New Testament

The New Testament of the Bible consists of twenty-seven different books. Nearly all these books were written in the first fifty years after the death and Resurrection of Jesus. Like the Old Testament books, they were written by various people in different circumstances and for different reasons. Also like the books of the Old Testament, God's Spirit brought them all together to tell one story: the story of Jesus Christ.

The books that make up the New Testament are not placed in the order in which they were written; rather, they are placed in order according to what type of book they are.

Gospels

The first four books are the Gospels of Matthew, Mark, Luke, and John. Each book is named after the man who wrote it. Each man told the story of Jesus: His ministry, death, and Resurrection. Although each writer is talking about the same Person, Jesus, each relates different parts of Jesus' life and Public Ministry that they either heard of or witnessed personally. This is one thing that makes the Gospels so interesting.

The Gospels are followed by another book of history called the Acts of the Apostles (or Acts). This book begins where the Gospels end—after Jesus rose from the dead. It tells how the Apostles chose Matthias to be Judas's successor. Acts relate the story of the thirty years after Jesus' life on earth. This book recounts how the Church began and how Christianity spread. Acts was written by Luke, the same man who wrote the Gospel of Luke.

A city gate in New Testament times. Notice the Roman soldiers, the traders and beggars, and the various animals.

The Roman Empire

"Buffer" state, protected by Rome

Roman Empire in A.D. 14

Letters

The next twenty-one books in the New Testament are letters, or epistles. Some are letters to people, while others are letters to churches or groups of believers. Fourteen have been attributed to Paul (formerly called Saul), a famous Apostle who once persecuted the Church. Paul's letters are placed in order according to length, from the longest to the shortest. There also are three letters by John (who wrote the Gospel of John), two letters by Peter (a fisherman and Apostle of Jesus who became the first Pope), one by James, and one by Jude. Although Hebrews was once thought to have been written by Paul, scholars are no longer sure of that. It speaks about Jesus, our High Priest, being the center of our lives.

Revelation

The last book of the New Testament is called Revelation. Revelation is an apocalyptic writing, meaning it teaches about God's plan through word pictures and visions that God gave to its writer, who identifies himself as John, probably referring to the author of the Gospel.

The New Testament teaches us how Jesus lived and how we should live. It relates the difficult situations churches can encounter and advises Christians how they should behave toward one another. The New Testament gives us hope that Jesus is coming again and that, one day, we will have a home with Him in heaven.

New Testament Timeline

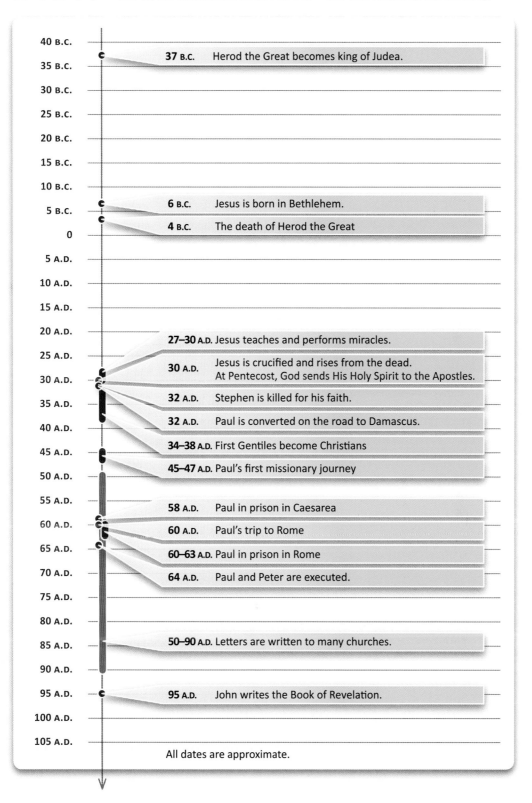

40 B.C.	
35 B.C.	**37 B.C.** Herod the Great becomes king of Judea.
30 B.C.	
25 B.C.	
20 B.C.	
15 B.C.	
10 B.C.	
5 B.C.	**6 B.C.** Jesus is born in Bethlehem.
0	**4 B.C.** The death of Herod the Great
5 A.D.	
10 A.D.	
15 A.D.	
20 A.D.	**27–30 A.D.** Jesus teaches and performs miracles.
25 A.D.	
30 A.D.	**30 A.D.** Jesus is crucified and rises from the dead. At Pentecost, God sends His Holy Spirit to the Apostles.
35 A.D.	**32 A.D.** Stephen is killed for his faith.
40 A.D.	**32 A.D.** Paul is converted on the road to Damascus.
45 A.D.	**34–38 A.D.** First Gentiles become Christians
50 A.D.	**45–47 A.D.** Paul's first missionary journey
55 A.D.	**58 A.D.** Paul in prison in Caesarea
60 A.D.	**60 A.D.** Paul's trip to Rome
65 A.D.	**60–63 A.D.** Paul in prison in Rome
70 A.D.	**64 A.D.** Paul and Peter are executed.
75 A.D.	
80 A.D.	
85 A.D.	**50–90 A.D.** Letters are written to many churches.
90 A.D.	
95 A.D.	**95 A.D.** John writes the Book of Revelation.
100 A.D.	
105 A.D.	

All dates are approximate.

The Life and Times of Jesus

Jesus is the main figure in the entire Bible. In the very first book of the Bible, God said someone would crush Satan; that was the first promise of salvation. Throughout the Old Testament, God's messengers, the prophets, tell of someone who would come to restore peace.

The New Testament is all about that Messiah, Jesus Christ. It tells about His birth, life, teachings, miracles, death, and Resurrection. It also tells about His followers and how they spread the Good News about Him.

The special Baby

Jesus came into the world like no other child before Him. A young Jewish woman named Mary was engaged to be married to a carpenter named Joseph. Mary was a virgin. Mary became pregnant by the power of God's Holy Spirit. Joseph was not the father—God was. Centuries before Jesus was born, God's messengers had foretold that God would send a Messiah Who would free us from our sins.

An angel told Mary she would give birth to God's Son. Later, an angel told Joseph that Mary was pregnant by the Spirit of God, and that he should not fear taking Mary as his wife. When Jesus was born, angels announced His birth to shepherds. Furthermore, wise men followed a star to find the new King of the Jews in Bethlehem. In the Temple, two people, advanced in years, who loved God, Simeon and Anna, recognized the Baby Jesus as the One whom God had promised long ago.

Joseph was a carpenter and Jesus learned his earthly father's trade. The Holy Family lived in Nazareth. In most ways, their family was like any other ordinary Jewish family there.

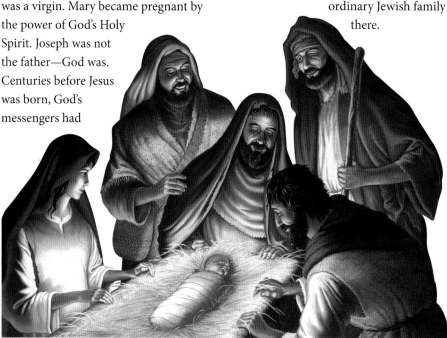

Shepherds come to visit the newborn Baby Jesus in the stable in Bethlehem.

When Jesus was twelve years old, He went to Jerusalem with His parents for Passover. Later, Mary and Joseph found Him talking with the religious teachers. Everyone was amazed at how much He knew and understood.

For many years Jesus worked as a carpenter. He appeared to be quite ordinary, but, when he was about thirty years old, things changed.

Jesus and John

Jesus had a cousin named John, who was called the "Baptist" or "Baptizer" because he baptized people in the River Jordan. John was preparing the way for the Messiah. When Jesus went to John to be baptized, John heard God say to Jesus, "You are my beloved Son; in You I am well pleased" (Luke 3:22).

After that, Jesus spent time in the desert where He prayed. He ate nothing for forty days. Satan tempted Him, trying to get Jesus to worship him and turn His back on God, but Jesus stood firm against the devil. He was ready to do the work that God had sent Him to do.

The teacher

Jesus began teaching people about God. The religious leaders had made a great many rules about how to worship God. They had made it burdensome for people to know God, so many just went through the motions of keeping the laws; others gave up completely.

Many people liked listening to Jesus. Crowds followed Him from town to town as He taught about God's love. Jesus always spent a great deal of time praying to the Father.

One day, He began to choose the twelve men who were to be His Apostles.

Jesus' cousin, John the Baptist, preached in the desert, calling on people to change their lives.

The men left their jobs. For three years, they lived and journeyed with Jesus. They listened to His teachings, watched His miracles, and asked questions. He told them that He was going to die and rise again, but they didn't understand what He was saying until after His death and Resurrection.

Jesus spoke to the people in parables—stories He took from everyday life. He told them what God's Kingdom is like. Jesus said that His followers should love their enemies and serve each other. He taught about God's love for people and spoke about forgiveness, purity, faithfulness in marriage, honesty, keeping promises, obeying God, getting rid of sin, being thankful, and many other things.

The healer

Besides teaching the people, Jesus showed His love and power by healing people who were blind, lame, mute, or had serious diseases. He fed large crowds of people (more than 5,000 at one time)

145

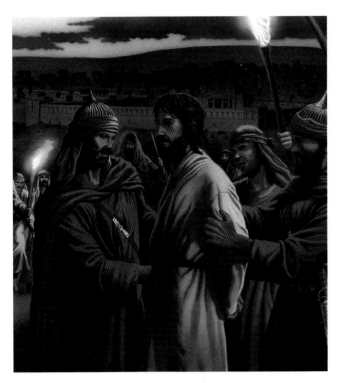

Jesus is arrested by the Temple guards in the Garden of Gethsemane.

with as little as two fish and five loaves of bread. He called demons out of people. He even raised from the dead Jairus's daughter, a widow's son, and Lazarus.

The friend

Unlike people of His time, who treated women and children like property, Jesus treated them with respect and kindness. In fact, He said that people had to become like children to enter God's Kingdom. When He was on the Cross, He made sure John would take care of His dear Mother.

Jesus, however, didn't get along with everyone. He criticized religious leaders for thinking they were better than others. Jesus angered them because He called God His Father, and He spent time with people they deemed to be sinners. Ultimately, the religious leaders came to hate Jesus so much that they had Him crucified.

God's plan

Actually, Jesus was born to die. God had planned it before time began. Jesus left His throne in heaven with the purpose of making a way for people to belong to God's family. Jesus was the only human being good enough to die for the sins of the world. Because He is God, He is perfect and sinless. He became a man so He could show people how to live. He died on the Cross to pay the penalty for the sins of the just and the unjust.

When the time came for Jesus to die, one of His own Apostles, Judas Iscariot, betrayed Him. Another, Simon Peter, denied even knowing Him. Except for John, the rest of the disciples deserted Him. Jesus knew all this was going to happen. In fact, the night before He was crucified, He prayed and asked the Father to protect His disciples. Jesus also prayed for all the people who would believe in Him in the future.

Jesus' death

Jesus was arrested at night and brought to trial. Since He had done nothing wrong, there was no proper evidence against Him. Yet, Jesus was slapped, mocked, and treated like a criminal. Pilate, a Roman official, wanted to let Jesus go, but the religious leaders led the crowd in calling for Him to be crucified. To avoid a riot, Pilate yielded and sent Jesus to be scourged and crucified.

Crucifixion was a painful, shameful death. In addition to the physical pain Jesus experienced, He shouldered the sin and guilt of all people for all time. As Jesus hung on the Cross, the sky grew dark. At His death, the veil of the sanctuary tore from top to bottom.

The risen Jesus appears to His disciples while they are fishing in the Sea of Galilee.

Besides His Mother and the Apostle John, only the women who had followed Jesus and ministered to him stayed at the Cross until He died. Joseph of Arimathea, who had been a secret follower of Jesus, asked Pilate for His body. Along with Nicodemus, another secret follower, he buried him in a tomb hewn out of rock.

Alive again!

In Luke's post-Resurrection account (Luke 24:1-11), early on Sunday morning, some of the women went to anoint Jesus' body. It was their way of showing care and respect for the dead. To their great surprise, the tomb was empty and two angels said that Jesus had risen—just as He had said He would.

The women ran to Jesus' Apostles. They tried to tell them the Good News about Jesus. At first, no one would believe them.

Later that evening, when Jesus appeared in the room where the disciples were, despite the door to the room being locked (according to John 20:19), they believed He had risen.

Jesus appeared to His disciples at different times before He ascended to heaven to prepare a place for His people to live for eternity. He promised to return one day and to take them to be with Him in heaven. No one knows when that will happen. Jesus has kept all His promises thus far, and He will surely keep this promise as well.

Jesus teaches His followers on a hillside near the Sea of Galilee. This famous teaching is called the Sermon on the Mount.

that Jesus is the One God promised. Matthew makes it clear that Joseph was Mary's husband and that Mary was Jesus' Mother, but that God was Jesus' Father. Joseph was Jesus' legal, or earthly, father. This showed that Jesus was in the royal line of King David.

The Gospel of Matthew is best known for Jesus' Sermon on the Mount (5—7) and the Great Commission (28:18–20). Besides these, there are other noteworthy texts in Matthew that have great meaning for people. They include the visit of the wise men, what Jesus said about the Law and the Kingdom of heaven, and Jesus' entry into Jerusalem on a donkey.

Four hundred years passed between the Book of Malachi, the last book in the Old Testament canon and the Gospel of Matthew, the first book in the New Testament canon. Divine revelation continued during this time, although there was a gap in prophetic revelation. Written by a disciple of Jesus, Matthew relates Jesus' life, teachings, Passion, death, and Resurrection.

This book is a good link between the Old and New Testaments. While it doesn't tell us everything Jesus did and said, it shows that Jesus fulfills the prophecies about the Messiah, the King of the Jews.

Matthew includes Jesus' genealogy, which extends back to Abraham, to show

Jesus came as King of the Jews. Yet, the people did not recognize Him because they thought He would set them free from the Romans. The Jews did not expect their King to be crucified—but Jesus rose from the dead, proving He is God's Son.

Afterward, He and the Father sent the Holy Spirit upon the Church to guide and protect it until the end of time.

OUTLINE

The outline of Matthew is very interesting. It alternates between Jesus' teachings and His miracles.

Jesus' birth (1—2)

Jesus is born in Bethlehem. The wise men come to worship Him, but this puts Jesus in danger, so His parents take Him to Egypt.

Jesus' Baptism and temptation (3—4)

Jesus is baptized by His cousin John the Baptist and tempted by Satan. Both events prepare Him for His task on earth.

Sermon on the Mount (5—7)

This is one of Jesus' most famous sermons and includes the Beatitudes.

Jesus shows His power (8—9)

Among other miracles, Jesus calms a storm, sends demons into a herd of pigs, heals a bleeding woman, and raises a girl from the dead.

Jesus trains and sends out the Apostles (10)

Jesus has called His Apostles and trained them. He now sends them out to do His work.

Jesus is rejected (11—12)

The Pharisees are jealous and scared of Jesus. They start challenging Him whenever they can.

Parables about growth (13)

Jesus teaches people by telling them stories. These stories are about a sower, a mustard seed, yeast, wheat and weeds, hidden treasure, a pearl, and a fishing net.

Jesus reveals His mission (14—17)

Jesus feeds more than 5,000 people with five loaves and two fish, walks on the water, is transfigured on a mountain, and rescues a boy from a demon. Peter declares that Jesus is the Messiah.

Jesus teaches about relationships (18)

Jesus tells the parables of the lost sheep and of an unmerciful servant who was tortured for his misdeed.

Jesus goes to Jerusalem (19—23)

Jesus answers questions, receives little children, tells more parables, heals more people, and enters Jerusalem on a donkey amid cheers.

Jesus teaches about the coming of the Kingdom (24—25)

Jesus tells about the last days and about when He will come back to earth as King.

Jesus' death and Resurrection (26:1—28:15)

Jesus says goodbye to His disciples and gives up His own life. God raises Him from the dead, and the disciples see Him again.

Jesus returns to heaven (28:16—20)

Jesus commands His Apostles to go and make disciples.

Matthew records that Mary and Joseph took Jesus to Egypt for safety.

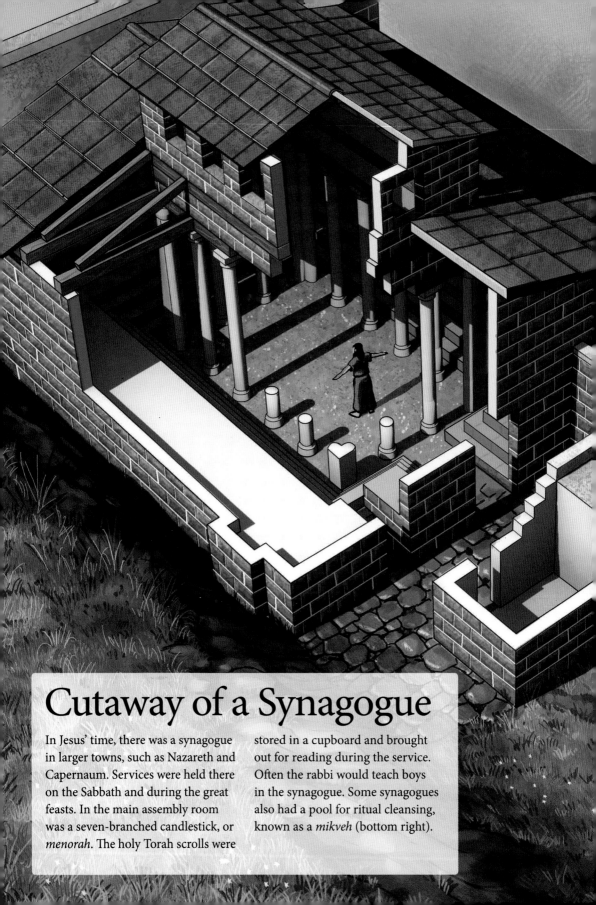

Cutaway of a Synagogue

In Jesus' time, there was a synagogue in larger towns, such as Nazareth and Capernaum. Services were held there on the Sabbath and during the great feasts. In the main assembly room was a seven-branched candlestick, or *menorah*. The holy Torah scrolls were stored in a cupboard and brought out for reading during the service. Often the rabbi would teach boys in the synagogue. Some synagogues also had a pool for ritual cleansing, known as a *mikveh* (bottom right).

Messiah

The Jewish people had been waiting for a Messiah. The Old Testament taught them that God would send someone to save them. The Jews thought God would send a mighty warrior who would fight for them against their enemies. They were disappointed when God's Messiah turned out to be a man who liked to teach them—not fight for them. Jesus was the Messiah they had been waiting for, and He will one day save us from all our enemies.

Look out for...

As you read Matthew, look out for...

Quotes from the Old Testament. *Matthew quotes the Old Testament more than fifty times and refers to it over seventy-five times.*

Words of Jesus. *Matthew relates many sermons and parables that Jesus told.*

Kingdom of heaven. *Matthew uses this phrase more than thirty times. Matthew presents Jesus as King.*

Frequently Asked Questions

Q: Why was it important to show that Jesus is the Messiah?
A: God made many promises in the Old Testament about the coming of the Messiah. In the New Testament, Jesus shows that God keeps His promises.

Q: What is the Sermon on the Mount?
A: The Sermon on the Mount is a very well-known part of Jesus' teaching. It includes the Beatitudes (5:3–12), the Lord's Prayer (6:9–13), and the Golden Rule (7:12).

Study Questions

- What did Jesus say about worry? (6:25–34)
- Who is the greatest in the Kingdom of heaven? (18:1–4)
- One of the most famous passages in the Bible is Matthew 28:16–20. What makes it so important?

The Miracles of Jesus

The first miracle Jesus performed was at a wedding in Cana, when He turned water into wine. After that, He performed many other miracles and became much more widely known. Here is a list of Jesus' miracles that are recorded in the Bible.

Healing of individuals

Healing an invalid
John 5:5–9

Healing a royal official's son
John 4:46–53

Healing a girl possessed by a demon
Matthew 15:22, 28; Mark 7:25, 29

Healing a man possessed by a demon
Mark 1:23–26; Luke 4:33–35

Healing a deaf mute
Mark 7:32–35

Healing Peter's mother-in-law
Matthew 8:14–15; Mark 1:30–31; Luke 4:38–39

Healing a blind man in Bethsaida
Mark 8:22–25

Healing a leper
Matthew 8:2–3; Mark 1:40–42; Luke 5:12–13

Healing a man who was born blind
John 9:6–7

Healing a paralyzed man
Matthew 9:2, 6–7; Mark 2:5, 10–12; Luke 5:20, 24–25

Healing a boy possessed by a demon
Matthew 17:18; Mark 9:25; Luke 9:42

Healing a man with a withered hand
Matthew 12:13; Mark 3:1, 5; Luke 6:6, 10

Healing a blind and mute man possessed by a demon
Matthew 12:22

Healing a centurion's servant
Matthew 8:5–13; Luke 7:1–10

Healing a woman who had been crippled for eighteen years
Luke 13:10–17

Raising a widow's son from the dead
Luke 7:14–15

Healing a man with dropsy
Luke 14:2–4

Healing a man possessed by demons at Gadara
Matthew 8:31–32; Mark 5:1–13; Luke 8:26–33

Raising Lazarus from the dead
John 11:43–44

Healing a bleeding woman
Matthew 9:22; Mark 5:27–29; Luke 8:43–44

Healing a blind man in Jericho
Mark 10:46–52; Luke 18:35–43

Raising Jairus's daughter from the dead
Matthew 9:25; Mark 5:41–42; Luke 8:54–55

Healing a man's severed ear
Luke 22:50–51

Healing a mute man possessed by a demon
Matthew 9:32–33

Miracles involving control of laws of nature

Changing water to wine
John 2:1–11

Catching many fish
Luke 5:4–7

Calming a stormy sea
Matthew 8:26; Mark 4:39; Luke 8:24–25

Feeding 5,000 people
*Matthew 14:13–21; Mark 6:30–44;
Luke 9:10–17; John 6:1–11*

Walking on the water
Matthew 14:25; Mark 6:48; John 6:19

Feeding 4,000 people
Matthew 15:32–38; Mark 8:6–10

Catching a fish with a coin in its mouth
Matthew 17:27

Destroying a fig tree
Matthew 21:19; Mark 11:13–14

Catching a great number of fish
John 21:5–6

Healing groups of people

Healing two blind men
Matthew 9:29–30

Healing ten men with leprosy
Luke 17:11–19

Healing a crowd in Capernaum
Mark 1:32–34

Healing a crowd by the Sea of Galilee
Mark 3:7–12

**Healing a crowd on a hillside by
the Sea of Galilee**
Matthew 15:29–31

KEY EVENTS
Jesus' travels

1. Bethlehem and Nazareth

Jesus was born in Bethlehem. His parents took Him to the Temple in Jerusalem to present Him to the Lord. Later, they fled to Egypt to escape King Herod's anger. When it was safe, they returned to Nazareth, where Jesus grew up. At the age of twelve, He went with His family to Jerusalem for Passover and debated with the religious leaders (Matthew 2:13–15; Luke 2:3-7; 22–24; 39–50).

2. River Jordan

Jesus was baptized in the River Jordan by His cousin John the Baptist. The Holy Spirit then led Jesus to the desert, where Satan tempted Him after forty days. Jesus answered the devil with Scripture and resisted His temptations. Jesus was ready for His life's work (Matthew 3:13–17; 4:1–11; Luke 3:21–22; 4:1–13).

3. Capernaum

Jesus spent the last three years of His life showing people signs of the Kingdom of God. He made His headquarters in Capernaum and journeyed through Israel, preaching, teaching, and healing the sick (Matthew 9:35). He called several of His disciples from their fishing nets on the Sea of Galilee. Near Capernaum, Jesus gave His Sermon on the Mount, including the Beatitudes (Matthew 5—7).

4. Nazareth

In His hometown of Nazareth, Jesus did not perform many miracles because people did not believe in Him (Matthew 13:53–58).

5. Sea of Galilee

By the Sea of Galilee, Jesus fed more than 5,000 people with just five loaves of bread and two fish (Matthew 14:13–21).

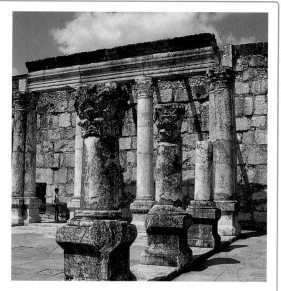

Restored remains of the third-century A.D. synagogue at Capernaum, which almost certainly stands on the site of the synagogue where Jesus taught

6. Tyre

In Tyre, a Gentile woman asked Jesus to heal her daughter. Jesus was amazed at her faith and did as she asked (Matthew 15:21–28).

7. Caesarea Philippi

At Caesarea Philippi, Jesus' disciple Peter first declared that Jesus was the Christ, the Son of God (Matthew 16:13–20).

8. Jericho

The tax collector Zacchaeus lived in Jericho. Jesus went to his house to bring him salvation (Luke 19:1–10).

9. Bethany

In Bethany, Jesus brought his friend Lazarus back to life (John 11:1–44).

10. Jerusalem

In Jerusalem, Jesus gave His life for the sin of the world, was buried, and was raised from the dead (John 18—21).

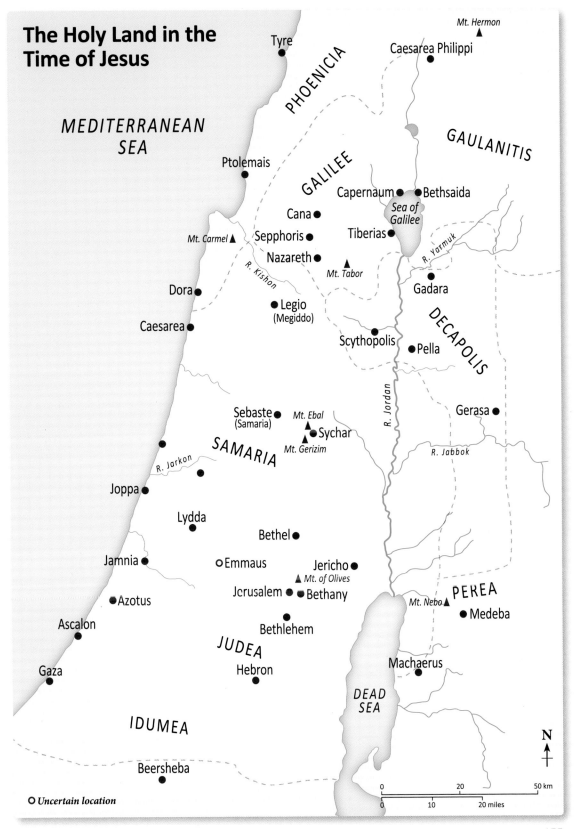

The Holy Land in the Time of Jesus

MEDITERRANEAN SEA

PHOENICIA

Tyre

Mt. Hermon ▲

Caesarea Philippi ●

GAULANITIS

Ptolemais ●

GALILEE

Capernaum ● ● Bethsaida

Sea of Galilee

Cana ●

Sepphoris ●

Tiberias ●

Mt. Carmel ▲

Nazareth ●

Mt. Tabor ▲

R. Kishon

R. Yarmuk

Gadara ●

Dora ●

Legio (Megiddo) ●

DECAPOLIS

Caesarea ●

Scythopolis ●

Pella ●

R. Jordan

Sebaste (Samaria) ●

Mt. Ebal ▲

Gerasa ●

SAMARIA

▲ ● Sychar

Mt. Gerizim

R. Jabbok

R. Jarkon

●

Joppa ●

Lydda ●

Bethel ●

Jamnia ●

○Emmaus

Jericho ●

▲ Mt. of Olives

PEREA

Jerusalem ● ● Bethany

Azotus ●

Mt. Nebo ▲ ● Medeba

Ascalon ●

Bethlehem ●

JUDEA

Machaerus ●

Gaza ●

Hebron ●

DEAD SEA

IDUMEA

N

Beersheba ●

○ *Uncertain location*

| 0 | | 20 | | 50 km |
| 0 | 10 | | 20 miles | |

Jerusalem in the Time of Jesus

Jerusalem occupied roughly the same area as in the time of Hezekiah, but it had expanded to the north and southwest. It was dominated by Herod's Temple, with its impressive courtyards and colonnades (below). Herod the Great had also built for himself a strongly fortified and towered palace (top left), where the Roman governor Pilate resided while in Jerusalem. We know the city also boasted a Roman arena and several pools. A gate from the Temple Mount led directly to the Mount of Olives, probably via a bridge across the Kidron Valley (below). During the great Jewish feasts, throngs of pilgrims visited the Temple.

MARK

Galilee in the Time of Jesus

Merom

GALILEE

Chorazin

Capernaum • Gamala

Gennesaret • Bethsaida

Magdala • SEA OF GALILEE • Gergesa

• Cana

Tiberias • • Hippos

• Sepphoris

R. Yarmuk

• Nazareth

▲ Mt. Tabor

• Nain

▲ Mt. Moreh

Gadara •

R. Jordan

to Jerusalem

DECAPOLIS

N

R. Harod

Action is the key word for the Gospel of Mark. Mark wrote his Gospel showing what Jesus did more than telling what He said. Mark wasn't a disciple of Jesus, but he received much of what he wrote about Jesus from the Apostle Peter. The Gospel of Mark may be the first of the New Testament books that was written.

Mark is the shortest of the four Gospels, yet, it has as many of Jesus' miracles as any of the other Gospels. Mark describes Jesus' life, death, burial, and Resurrection. He often pictures Jesus as a servant.

Mark was writing to people who were Christians of non-Jewish origin. They were Romans, Syrians, Greeks, and others who didn't know about the coming of the Messiah. Jesus' actions in helping the sick and needy were meaningful for these people. When Jesus healed people from terrible diseases, they could see He had come from the Father.

Jesus wanted to show God's love to people so they would believe in Him.

OUTLINE

Jesus is popular in Galilee (1:1—3:12)

John the Baptist prepares the way for Jesus and brings Him into the spotlight. Jesus begins to gather disciples and heal people.

Jesus makes friends and enemies (3:13—7:23)

The Jewish leaders begin to dislike Jesus. They are afraid He will become more important than they are.

Jesus and His disciples (7:24—9:50)

Jesus continues to heal people and spends a good deal of time teaching the disciples and preparing them for the work they are to do as His followers.

Jesus goes to Judea (10)

Jesus travels to the south. He blesses children and heals more people.

Death and Resurrection of Jesus (11—16)

Jesus returns to Jerusalem. He confronts the Jewish leaders and has His Last Supper with the Apostles. He is then crucified. Three days later, He rises from the dead.

All four Gospels recount Jesus' entry into Jerusalem on a donkey. The people waved palms and greeted Him loudly and joyfully.

Look out for...

As you read Mark, look out for...

Explanations. *Mark may have written this Gospel for Christians who were not Jews. Because of this, he explains Jewish traditions and customs.*

Miracles. *Mark records twenty of the thirty-five miracles that Jesus performed.*

"Immediately." *More than forty times, Mark uses a word that means "immediately" or "right away."*

Frequently Asked Questions

Q: Why did Mark write his Gospel especially for non-Jewish people?
A: The Holy Spirit inspired people to write the Word of God to meet the needs of different people. The Romans, Syrians, Greeks, and others who were not Jewish might not have understood all the history and promises that God had made to the Jews (see the Gospel of Matthew). They could, however, understand God's love shown through Jesus' actions.

Q: How did Jesus treat people who were not God's chosen people, the Jews?
A: Jesus wanted everyone to experience God's love and forgiveness. He showed that God cares for Jews and non-Jews alike by healing them, casting out demons, going to their towns and preaching, and sending His disciples to serve them.

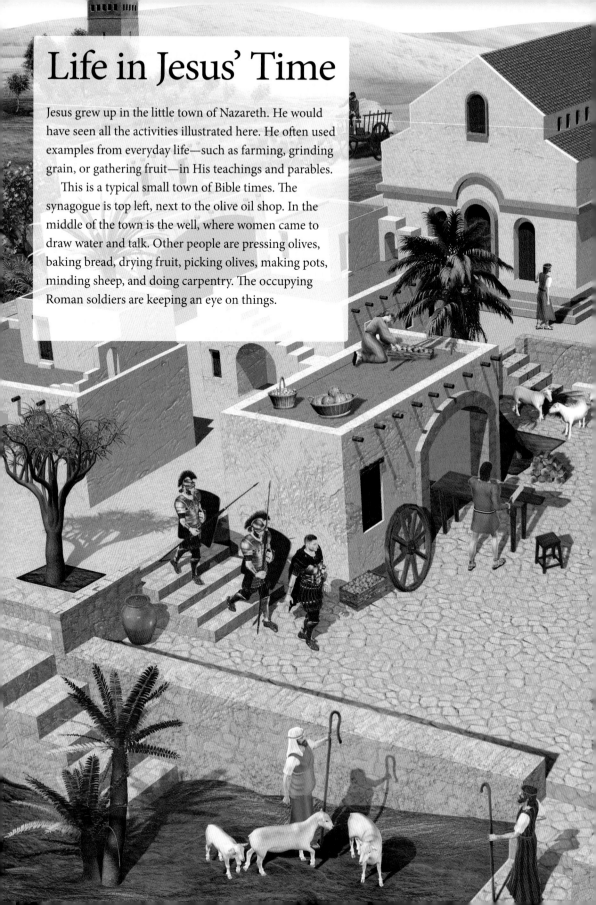

Life in Jesus' Time

Jesus grew up in the little town of Nazareth. He would have seen all the activities illustrated here. He often used examples from everyday life—such as farming, grinding grain, or gathering fruit—in His teachings and parables.

This is a typical small town of Bible times. The synagogue is top left, next to the olive oil shop. In the middle of the town is the well, where women came to draw water and talk. Other people are pressing olives, baking bread, drying fruit, picking olives, making pots, minding sheep, and doing carpentry. The occupying Roman soldiers are keeping an eye on things.

The Resurrection

This ancient tomb in Jerusalem has a rolling stone door that is similar to the door used to seal Jesus' body in the tomb of Joseph of Arimathea (Luke 23:50–55).

Mark's Gospel ends with the exciting story of the Resurrection. Jesus had died on the Cross. He had been buried in a stone tomb with a very heavy rock rolled in front of the opening. Mark tells us that three women came to this tomb and found the stone rolled away and an angel nearby. The angel told them Jesus was alive and had gone from the tomb.

The Resurrection of Jesus is the most important fact in Christian history. Jesus died for our sins, but the fact that He came back to life means He is greater than that sin and greater than death. Because Jesus rose from the dead, we who believe in Him will live forever.

Study Questions

- How did the "Ten Towns" (Decapolis) learn about Jesus' great power and care for people? (5:1–20)
- What did Jesus do for the many people who came to Him with problems? (6:53–56)
- How does Jesus want us to pray? (11:20–25)

LUKE

The devout elderly man Simeon greets Baby Jesus as the Lord's Messiah in Jerusalem (2:22–35).

Angels, shepherds, a stable, and a Baby—what could these things mean but Christmas? This best-known and most-loved Bible story comes from the Gospel of Luke.

Luke, the man who wrote this Gospel, was a Greek doctor. He provides many details about Jesus' birth and childhood not given by any of the other Gospels. His Gospel shows how Jesus was the perfect Man. It's clear that Jesus is God's Son because of the angel's announcement to Mary, but Luke also calls Jesus the Son of Man.

Matthew, Mark, and Luke are called the Synoptic Gospels. Synoptic, from the Greek, means "to see together." All three tell about Jesus, but each from a slightly different angle.

Luke has some details that the other Gospels do not have. For example, Luke records several joyful songs of praise. One of these is Mary's song, known as the *Magnificat*, which praises God for what He was going to do for her and through her.

Several parables of Jesus are found only in Luke. They give a clear picture of God's love for the lost. The Gospel of Luke also shows Jesus' tender care for women, who were often mistreated. We learn much about Jesus from the Gospel of Luke that would be unknown without it.

Luke, author of Luke's Gospel and the Acts of the Apostles, was a physician.

A nighttime view of Bethlehem, David's city, and the birthplace of Jesus

Frequently Asked Questions

Q: Why is it important that Jesus was a man?

A: He needed to be a perfect and sinless person to pay for the sins of all people. He faced temptation, just as we do, and He showed us what God is like and how God wants us to live.

Q: What did the angel tell Mary?

A: God sent the angel Gabriel to tell Mary she was to conceive and bear a Son. He, however, would not be an ordinary Baby born in an ordinary way. The Holy Spirit would come upon her and the power of God would overshadow her. Furthermore, Mary would remain a virgin.

OUTLINE

Jesus' birth, childhood, and roots (1—3)

Luke gives us information about the young Jesus that we cannot find elsewhere.

Jesus teaches and heals in Galilee (4—9)

Jesus teaches and heals around His hometown of Nazareth.

Jesus goes to Jerusalem (10—21)

Jesus leaves His home for Jerusalem, the religious capital for His people. The rest of His life is spent there.

Jesus dies on the Cross (22—24)

Jesus gives up His life and God raises Him from the dead, just as Jesus said He would.

Cleopas and his companion recognize the risen Christ as He breaks bread at supper in the village of Emmaus, outside Jerusalem (24:13–35).

The humanity of Christ

Jesus was God, but He also was one hundred percent human. This is hard for us to understand, which is why we call God's humanity a mystery. Luke's Gospel points out repeatedly that Jesus is human.

Luke tells about Jesus' early years, when He grew up as all humans do. Luke shows us Jesus' loving care for people as He healed the sick.

Jesus experienced life as do all humans, with happiness and sadness. He also was God, and He gave His life to redeem us.

Look out for...

As you read Luke, look out for...

Women. *Luke mentions more women than any other Gospel-writer (Evangelist).*

The poor. *Luke records many of Jesus' words concerning the poor.*

Prayers. *Several prayers are included in the Gospel of Luke.*

Songs. *Luke includes several songs, including Mary's, Zechariah's, and the angels' song to the shepherds in the countryside nearby Bethlehem.*

In a parable, Jesus used the familiar activity of sowing seed to teach His followers (8:4–15).

Study Questions

- What are some of the ways in which Jesus showed His special care for women? (7:11–15; 7:36–50; 13:10–17)
- How did Jesus treat children? (18:15–17)

The Parables of Jesus

Lessons from nature

The sower and four types of soil
Matthew 13:3–8, 18–23;
Mark 4:3–8, 14–20; Luke 8:5–8, 11–15

The weeds among the wheat
Matthew 13:24–30, 36–43

The fishing net
Matthew 13:47–50

The tiny mustard seed
Matthew 13:31–32; Mark 4:30–32;
Luke 13:18–19

The seed grows by itself
Mark 4:26–29

The seed that died
John 12:24

Yeast
Matthew 13:33; Luke 13:20–21

Signs of the future from a fig tree
Matthew 24:32–35; Mark 13:28–31;
Luke 21:29–33

The barren fig tree
Luke 13:6–9

The birds of heaven
Matthew 6:26–30

The vultures gather
Luke 17:37

The tree and its fruit
Matthew 7:16

The weather signs
Luke 12:54–56

Jobs and money

The good shepherd
John 10:1–5, 7–18

Wise and foolish builders
Matthew 7:24–27; Luke 6:47–49

The master and the servant
Luke 17:7–10

The wise and wicked servants
Matthew 24:45–51; Luke 12:42–48

Servants must be watchful
Mark 13:35–37; Luke 12:35–38

Workers in the vineyard
Matthew 20:1–16

The talents
Matthew 25:14–30; Luke 19:12–27

The lampstand
Matthew 5:14–16; Mark 4:21–23;
Luke 8:16–18, 11:33

The lamp of the body
Matthew 6:22–23

Salt that's thrown away
Matthew 5:13

New cloth on an old coat
Matthew 9:16; Mark 2:21; Luke 5:36

New wine in old wineskins
Matthew 9:17; Mark 2:22; Luke 5:37–38

Hidden treasure
Matthew 13:44

A valuable pearl
Matthew 13:45–46

Treasure from a storeroom
Matthew 13:52

The dishonest manager
Luke 16:1–12

The unforgiving servant
Matthew 18:23–35

The rich man who foolishly built
larger barns
Luke 12:16–21

The rich man and Lazarus
Luke 16:19–31

Wicked renters of a vineyard
Matthew 21:33–44; Mark 12:1–11;
Luke 20:9–18

JOHN

Jesus met the Pharisee Nicodemus by night. He explained to him, "For God so loved the world that He gave His only Son, so that everyone who believes in Him may not perish but may attain eternal life" (3:16, NCV).

Many people say Jesus never claimed to be God. It is clear that they never read the Gospel of John, written by John, one of Jesus' closest disciples.

John was with Jesus more than almost any other person. John was in Jesus' inner circle of friends and saw miracles that few others saw. He saw Jesus' glory when He was transfigured on a mountain. John heard God the Father say, "This is My beloved Son, with Whom I am well pleased. Listen to him" (Matthew 17:5). There is no uncertainty about John's message: Jesus is the Son of God.

From the beginning, John lets his readers know that Jesus was the Word of God. Jesus is a separate Person from the Father, and He is God. Through Jesus, all things came into existence.

John reports what Jesus taught about Himself. When Jesus talked about Himself using the words "I am," He was using words that God used in the Old Testament. Jesus said, "I am the bread of life… the light of the world… the gate… the good shepherd." Jesus was telling people that He is the One Who can meet their deepest needs. He is the only One Who can forgive sins and bring people into God's family.

John was at the Cross when Jesus died. He also was one of the first to see the empty tomb after Jesus rose from the dead.

Anyone who wants to know Who Jesus is can read an eyewitness report in the Gospel of John.

The Sea of Galilee at sundown

OUTLINE

The Word of Life (1:1–18)

John has a beautiful and almost poetic beginning to his Gospel, tracing Jesus' roots all the way back to God Himself. This is because John's purpose was to reveal Jesus as the Son of God.

Jesus reveals Who He is (1:19—6:71)

Jesus reveals Himself by calling His disciples, performing miracles, clearing merchants out of the Temple, talking to Nicodemus, talking to a Samaritan woman, and walking on water.

Jesus and the Jews (7—12)

Jesus had some enemies among the Jewish leaders. Yet, He still tried to explain to them that He was there to help them. He even raised Lazarus from the dead.

Jesus and His disciples (13—17)

Jesus spends some time alone with the disciples. He teaches them and eats His last meal with them.

Jesus dies and rises again (18—21)

Jesus is betrayed by Judas and arrested. He is crucified and buried. He then rises from the dead and spends more time with His followers before He returns to heaven.

Jesus' last days in Jerusalem

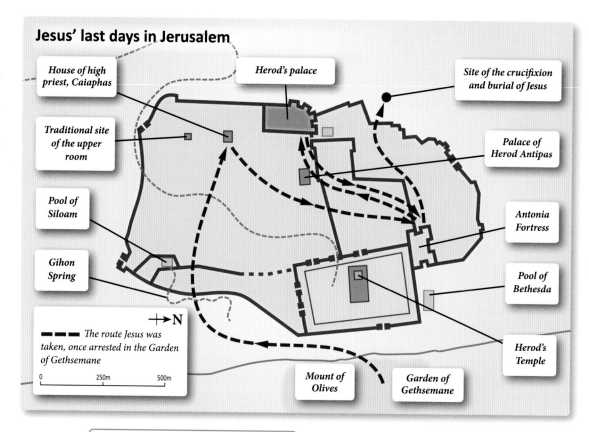

House of high priest, Caiaphas

Herod's palace

Site of the crucifixion and burial of Jesus

Traditional site of the upper room

Palace of Herod Antipas

Pool of Siloam

Antonia Fortress

Gihon Spring

Pool of Bethesda

N

Herod's Temple

■ ■ ■ The route Jesus was taken, once arrested in the Garden of Gethsemane

0   250m   500m

Mount of Olives

Garden of Gethsemane

Look out for...

As you read John, look out for...

Jesus as God. *John says clearly several times that Jesus is God.*

Key words. *John often uses the following key words: witness, believe (almost a hundred times), light, and love.*

The Holy Spirit. *John is the only Gospel that teaches much about the Holy Spirit.*

Word pictures. *John uses word pictures not employed by the other Gospels. For example, he calls Jesus the bread of life; the good shepherd; the light of the world; and the way, and the truth, and the life.*

Frequently Asked Questions

Q: What does "transfigured" mean?
A: It means that Jesus suddenly looked different. Even though Jesus was God while He was on earth, people did not see His glory. When Jesus was transfigured, His face shone and His clothes became dazzling white. Even though John does not report the Transfiguration, he speaks quite often of Jesus' glory.

Q: If the Book of Genesis says that God created the world, how can Jesus be the Creator?
A: Because Jesus is God.

Q: Why doesn't John recount everything that Jesus did?
A: None of the Gospel-writers tells us everything Jesus did; each gives us a picture of Jesus to show that He is God's Son, the Messiah.

Incarnation

Jesus was a human being like any other human. If He grazed His knee, it bled. He had feelings. He had to learn to read and write. Yet, through a miracle that only God understands, Jesus also was God. God came to live as a human being; this is the meaning of Incarnation.

This is the only time God has done this. He did it so that we can see that He wants to have a relationship with us. He wants that so much that He endured the punishment for our sins by dying on the Cross. That was His part in the relationship.

Our part is to believe in Him and to trust that He will do what He says. When we pray, we are showing that we believe He is listening and that He will answer. John wrote His Gospel so that we would believe in Jesus.

Study Questions

- What did another man named John say about Jesus? (1:29–34)
- How did Jesus' first miracle help His disciples believe in Him? (2:1–11)
- What did Jesus pray for Himself? (17:1–5)
- What did Jesus pray for His disciples and all future believers? (17:6–26)

Roman soldiers gamble for Jesus' robe while He suffers on the Cross. Pilate ordered that a notice saying, "Jesus the Nazorean, King of the Jews" be put on the Cross, overruling the chief priests' objections.

Herod's Temple

Herod the Great started to build the Temple in 20 B.C. The central Temple building, like the Tabernacle, consisted of a Holy Place and a Most Holy Place, though the latter no longer contained the Ark of the Covenant.

The two areas were divided by a great curtain, which was torn in two when Jesus died. As with Solomon's Temple, a huge altar of burnt sacrifice stood in front of the Temple.

The Temple was surrounded by a number of courts, each more exclusive than the last. Gentiles were only admitted into the outer courtyard. The inner Court of the Women (below) was lit by four huge lampstands.

ACTS

After his conversion, Paul escaped his enemies in Damascus by being let down from the city walls in a basket.

Whatever happened to the frightened disciples who ran off into the night when Jesus was arrested? The Acts of the Apostles tells the story. It tells what happened after the risen Christ appeared to them and sent the Holy Spirit to help them spread the Good News. It tells of the incredible events that followed after Jesus returned to heaven.

Acts is the history of the early Church. It tells how the Church began and how it grew and spread from Jerusalem to the Roman world.

The frightened disciples became brave spokesmen for Christ. They spoke to the religious leaders. They endured prison, beatings, and even death. Jesus' message of eternal life in God's family continued to spread.

A highly educated Jewish leader named Saul was told by Jesus that he was persecuting Him. The Lord then turned Saul's life upside down. Also known as Paul, he traveled far and wide to teach people about Jesus.

In addition to history, Acts tells what the Holy Spirit taught the Christians. The changed lives of the disciples and of many others, as recorded in Acts, give proof that Jesus Christ is Who He said He was—the Son of God.

The Spread of the Gospel

Pentecost

Pentecost was a Jewish feast that happened fifty days after the Passover. Jesus had been crucified at Passover and was then raised to life. He had appeared to His disciples and then returned to heaven. It was at this feast that the Holy Spirit, the Comforter, first came to live in God's people.

It is important to remember that in the time of Acts, the Church was changing fast. God's people were used to praying in the Temple, but Jesus had shown them that God was not just in the Temple. He was in them. They were used to offering sacrifices, but Jesus' death was the final sacrifice anyone would ever need. The coming of the Holy Spirit at Pentecost showed the early Church that from then on things would be different.

Frequently Asked Questions

Q: Who were Jesus' brothers?
A: Catholics, holding firm to the fact that Mary was always a virgin, understand the term "brothers of Jesus" to be his cousins.

Q: Why was the day of Pentecost so important?
A: This was the day the Holy Spirit came and filled the followers of Jesus, the first Christians. There was a noise like a loud, rushing wind. Then there were what looked like tongues of fire that rested on each person. They all began to speak in languages they didn't know. Those listening could understand, and many of them became Christians, too.

Paul's Missionary Travels

Paul's First Missionary Journey

Paul, Barnabas, and John Mark were sent west by the church in Antioch. After a while, John Mark left them. Paul always took his message to the Jews first, but usually they didn't want to hear about Jesus. Paul then would speak to the Gentiles. Paul's life was often in danger. With many Gentiles becoming believers, the Church had to decide if they first had to become Jews. Paul taught that faith is what makes someone a Christian—not keeping the Law (13—14).

Paul's Second Missionary Journey

Barnabas wanted to take John Mark again, but Paul didn't. They disagreed and went their separate ways. Paul instead took Silas with him to visit the believers in some of the towns he had visited on his first journey. Paul met many people who became his lifelong fellow believers and friends. Best known are Timothy, Lydia, Priscilla, and Aquila. Paul had a vision of a man in Macedonia, asking Paul to help his people; he did. On this journey, Paul and Silas were unjustly jailed; God sent an earthquake to rescue them. As a result, the jailer and his family became Christians (15:36—18:22).

Paul's Third Missionary Journey

Paul returned a third time to the cities he had visited before. Many of his New Testament letters are to churches in these cities. Paul's third journey was to address misunderstandings the believers had (18:23—20:38). In Ephesus, some men who were silversmiths and made idols of the goddess Artemis caused a riot to make Paul stop talking about God. Paul said farewell to the elders of the Ephesian church before returning to Jerusalem to report what God had done among the Gentiles (19:1—21:26).

Paul's Journey to Rome

When Paul returned to Jerusalem, he was arrested. Realizing that he could not obtain a fair trial in Jerusalem, he appealed to Caesar and was sent to Rome. After an eventful voyage, during which he was shipwrecked near Malta, he finally reached the imperial capital, where he eventually was executed (27:1—28:31).

Part of the Roman aqueduct shown in the illustration below is still visible on the beach at Caesarea.

Caesarea

At Caesarea, on the Mediterranean coast of Palestine, Herod the Great constructed the first artificial port of the ancient world. At the entrance stood a lighthouse.

The aqueduct that supplied fresh water to the Roman port is still visible. The city was named for Caesar Augustus and included a hippodrome, an amphitheater,

and a palace for Herod built on a promontory south of the harbor. The Roman governor of Palestine resided here most of the year.

Look out for...

As you read Acts, look out for...

The Holy Spirit. *Christians receive the gift of the Holy Spirit, just as Jesus had promised them.*

Decisions of the early Church. *The Church leaders have to make many decisions about how they will lead and how they will organize the Church.*

Study Questions

- What were Jesus' final instructions to His disciples? (1:8)
- How did God use an earthquake to save a family? (16:16–34)

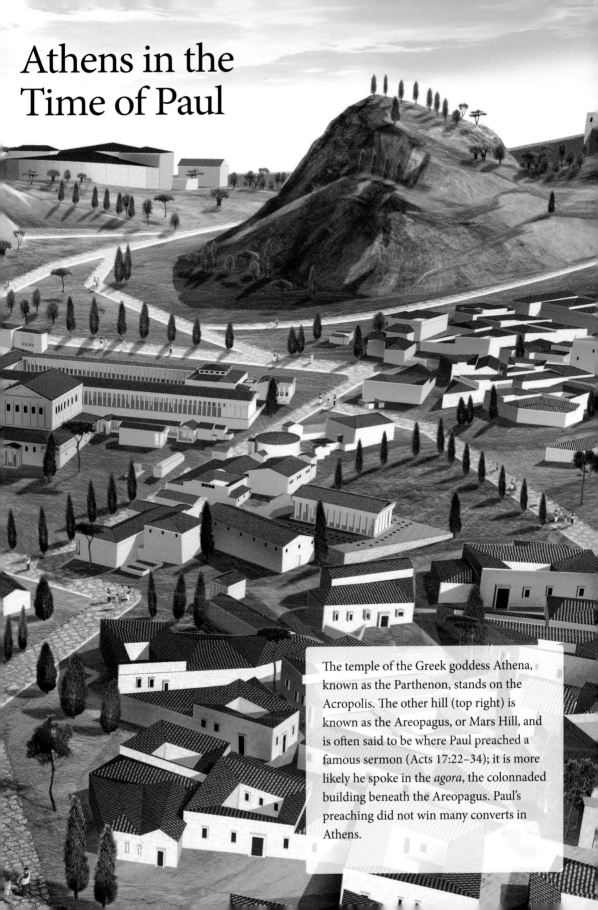

Athens in the Time of Paul

The temple of the Greek goddess Athena, known as the Parthenon, stands on the Acropolis. The other hill (top right) is known as the Areopagus, or Mars Hill, and is often said to be where Paul preached a famous sermon (Acts 17:22–34); it is more likely he spoke in the *agora*, the colonnaded building beneath the Areopagus. Paul's preaching did not win many converts in Athens.

ROMANS

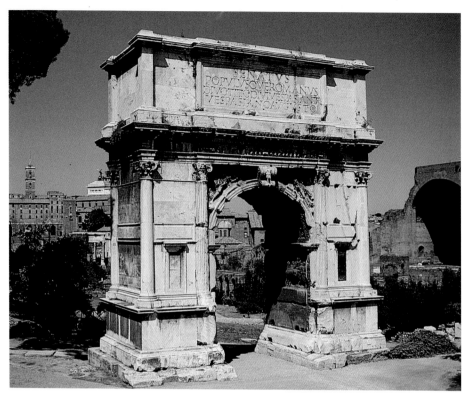

Titus's Arch, Rome, which was built to celebrate Titus's victories, including the siege of Jerusalem, A.D. 70. A panel inside the arch depicts the spoils taken from Herod's Temple before it was destroyed.

The Apostle Paul had never met the people in the church at Rome, but he had heard about them. He hoped to visit the Christians in Rome on a voyage he planned. He wanted to introduce himself and explain the Christian faith to the Roman believers. He wrote to them about what it means to be a Christian.

The letter, or epistle, that Paul wrote to them is called Romans. It clearly explains that everyone has sinned because everyone is descended from Adam. It relates the Good News that Jesus Christ died and rose again to pay the penalty for our sin.

Even though we have sinned and fully deserve to be condemned because of what we have done, God treats us more like a loving parent than a vengeful judge. In fact, God redefines justice as mercy.

Romans also tells about Israel, the Church, spiritual gifts, faith, and the Christian life.

Other things people can learn from Romans are that Christ can free us from sin, help us to be like Himself, and help us live to please Him.

OUTLINE

Why Paul is writing (1:1–17)

Paul says he is writing to the Romans to explain the gospel, and what it means for their everyday lives.

We live in a lost world (1:18—3:20)

Paul writes to the Romans about the Jewish world as well as the Gentile world. He says both worlds need the gospel.

We are accepted by God by faith, not good works (3:21—5:21)

Paul talks about many different truths here, but this is his main theme.

Live holy lives (6—8)

Even though we have been accepted by God through our faith, we still have to work to keep sin out of our lives.

The Jews (9—11)

God made some important promises to the Jews, and He is going to keep those promises. The Jews have a special heritage—but salvation is for everyone, not just for the Jews.

Christian conduct (12:1—15:13)

As Christians, we are God's representatives. We need to live lives that please Him.

Notes from Paul (15:14—16:27)

It is good to remember that this actually is a letter. At the end, Paul shares news with his readers and greets friends in Rome.

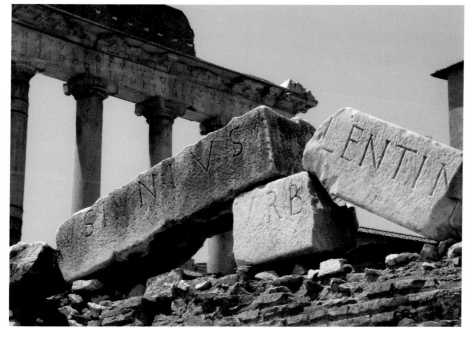

Inscribed stones in the ruins of the Forum, Rome

The Forum, Rome, by night

Look out for...

As you read Romans, look out for...

Faith. *Paul talks a great deal about faith, because many people still thought that if they kept enough rules they could please God in that way instead of through faith.*

Sin. *Paul tells us the truth about sin: we all do wrong, and we need God's forgiveness.*

Abraham. *Abraham is an important person in this epistle because he is an example to us all. Abraham did many admirable things that pleased God, but it was his faith that gladdened God greatly.*

Justification by faith

Justification means to be at peace with God. We are justified when we trust in the love that God showed us in Jesus' death on the Cross.

God is holy. He is not like anything or anyone else. He has no evil, no wrong, and no sin in Him. Paul's question to the Romans was: "How can we, a sinful people, be justified (become righteous) to a holy, sinless God?" Paul's answer was: "By our faith in Christ."

When we believe in God, in His Son, Jesus, and in Jesus' death and Resurrection, we are giving God exactly what He wants—our faith. We believe Him. We believe in Him. That is what He asks of us. We are justified by our faith.

Paul under armed escort by Roman soldiers in the capital city, Rome

Frequently Asked Questions

Q: How did the people in Rome become Christians?

A: First and foremost, St. Peter, the first Pope, established the Church in Rome. It is also true that Romans may have heard the gospel from some Jews who had been in Jerusalem during Pentecost. When Peter and Jesus' other disciples received the Holy Spirit, they spoke freely about Christ. Many people heard the gospel and believed in Jesus. They then took the Good News home with them.

Q: What does Adam's sin have to do with people now?

A: Adam is the father of all people. We all have inherited his sinful nature. Even very good people cannot be good all the time and in every way.

Q: How can anyone be good enough to go to heaven?

A: No one but Jesus is good enough to go to heaven. That is why He died in our place and why we need to trust Him. He gives us His goodness and helps us do what is good and right.

Study Questions

- How did Paul praise the Lord? (11:33–36)
- Since Jesus forgives sins, how should people behave? (12:1–21)

Rome in the Time of Paul

Rome is famously built on seven hills and on the Tiber River. Prominent in the illustration is the great hippodrome, venue for the celebrated chariot races, other sporting events, and where many early Christians were martyred. The Colosseum (the circular building top middle) was built after Paul's death. Many Roman temples are also shown, as well as the Theater of Marcellus (far left) beside the river.

1 CORINTHIANS

The impressive columns of the Temple of Apollo, Corinth

The Apostle Paul was like a father to the Christians in Corinth. He lived in that city for many months during his second missionary journey. Paul told people how Jesus died and rose again to save them from sin. Many of them believed and became Christians. First Corinthians is a letter that Paul wrote to his spiritual children in Corinth.

He wrote it from Ephesus during his third missionary journey. After Paul left Corinth, the people had problems putting their Christian faith into practice. They wrote to him asking for advice. Paul wrote 1 Corinthians to answer their questions and to give them more instructions.

Corinth was a large city by the sea. It had a temple to the goddess Aphrodite. There was a good deal of idol-worship, wealth, greed, and immorality in Corinth. Before some of the people became Christians, they lived sinful lives like those around them. After becoming Christians, they were not sure how to live.

Paul thus wrote about topics that would help them, such as Christian unity, purity, marriage, spiritual gifts, worship, and future resurrection. He also addressed his letter to "all those everywhere who call on the name of our Lord Jesus Christ" (1:2b, NCV), so that others would learn from it. Christians now and in the future also can learn from the advice and teaching in 1 Corinthians.

Corinth in the Time of Paul

Like Athens, Corinth was dominated by a steep hill, known as Acrocorinth. The city itself boasted all the features of a Greek city of its time, including an amphitheater and smaller odeion; the columns of its Temple of Apollo (center) still stand. The forum, the center of government of the city and marketplace, is the large enclosed space, middle left. In its center is the judgment seat, or bema, where Paul was probably tried before Gallio (Acts 18:12).

OUTLINE

Problems Paul has heard about (1—6)

Paul criticizes the Corinthians' arguments, immorality, lawsuits against each other, and lack of wisdom.

Problems the Corinthians had written to Paul about (7—14)

Paul answers questions about marriage, food, the celebration of the Eucharist, and spiritual gifts.

Resurrection and eternal life (15)

Paul explains the Resurrection of Jesus and the resurrection of believers that will happen when Christ comes again.

Personal matters (16)

Paul gives instructions about Christian giving. He also sends them news about people they both know.

Look out for...

As you read 1 Corinthians, look out for...

Correction. Paul is writing to correct the Corinthians and help them rid their church of sin.

Sins of the body. Paul points out many different ways we should be careful with our bodies, especially the food we eat and the way we deal with sex.

Frequently Asked Questions

Q: What are spiritual gifts?
A: Spiritual gifts are special talents or abilities that God gives to Christians. Their purpose is to bring glory to God and to help other people. The Holy Spirit enables people to use their gifts. Spiritual gifts include teaching, serving, faith, healing, miraculous powers, and prophecy.

Q: Why did Paul talk about Jesus' Resurrection?
A: Some people thought Jesus never really died. Others doubted that He came alive again. Paul made it clear that Jesus died, was buried, and rose again, just as the Bible said He would. Paul said that Jesus appeared to Peter, the rest of the disciples, and then to more than 500 people at the same time. Jesus also appeared to His brother James and, finally, to Saul (Paul). If Jesus had not risen from the dead, we would not be able to be forgiven for our sins.

Immorality

If something is immoral, it simply is wrong or goes against the rules. The Corinthians were involved in immorality. Some of their sins were sexual sins. They also were immoral in the way they treated each other. They were not loving or kind, even taking each other to a court of law instead of working out their differences.

Paul wrote to them about their immorality so they would change their ways. He told them not to accept immorality in any way. Christians need to have high standards for their lives.

Study Questions

• What is so special about the gospel? (1:18–25)
• What is Paul's teaching on the Eucharist in this letter? (10—11)
• Why should a Christian show respect to every other Christian? (12:4–26)
• When is a Christian at his or her best? (Chapter 13)
• How does Paul describe the resurrected bodies that Christians will have? (15:42–57)

2 CORINTHIANS

It can be daunting to defend yourself against critics. The Apostle Paul was not fond of doing so either. He wrote 2 Corinthians to prove that God had called him to be an Apostle, just as He had called the original Twelve.

This letter was written within a year of 1 Corinthians. Instead of talking about Christian beliefs, it tells of Paul's life and service. It is a very personal letter, telling us how Paul felt about the problems he was facing. There were false teachers in Corinth who were trying to discredit Paul and his message about Jesus.

OUTLINE

Paul's work for Jesus (1—7)
Paul thanks God for His consololation during hardship and tells the Corinthians about some of his decisions.

Gifts (8—9)
The benefits of giving generously and a reminder of what the Corinthians have promised to do.

Paul defends himself against false apostles (10—12)
Paul states his authority and attacks the false teachers who have lied about him.

Closing matters (13)
Paul gives some final advice.

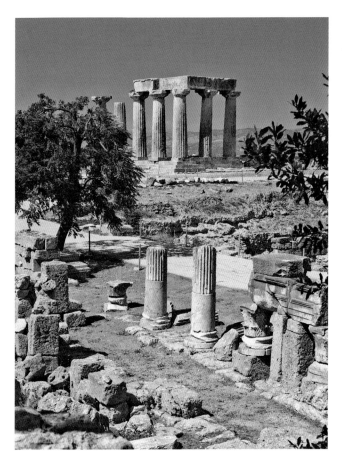

Even though Paul did not want to defend himself, he reminded the Corinthians of how God had used him to bring them to Christ. He told them how he had suffered for Jesus in order to share the gospel with them.

The Corinthian believers were still immature in many ways. Paul encouraged them to believe the truth—instead of believing the false teachers. He did not want to find them living sinful lives the next time he visited them. He loved them and wanted them to live in fellowship with the Lord Jesus.

Another view of the ruins of ancient Corinth. Paul had a great deal to say to the Christians in Corinth.

Look out for...

As you read 2 Corinthians, look out for...

Personal news. This is a very personal letter by Paul. If you read it carefully, you can learn a great deal about him from the things he says about himself.

Difficult times. Paul talks about many of his own difficulties and how God has helped him through them.

Thorn in the flesh

We do not know what Paul meant in chapter 12 by his "thorn in the flesh." We do know that it was something wrong with him. He prayed for God to take it away, but God did not. Because of some of the things Paul says in other places, it may have been a problem with his eyes. It affected his appearance as well as caused him pain.

Paul, however, did not let his "thorn in the flesh" hold him back. He still loved people and served them. People sometimes say, "That's my thorn in the flesh." Yet, it shouldn't be an excuse for giving up. Paul's thorn never stopped him.

Paul writes to his Christian friends.

Frequently Asked Questions

Q: How did Paul suffer?
A: Paul suffered beatings, imprisonment, riots, hard work, sleepless nights, and hunger. He even had to be lowered over a city wall in a large basket to escape from his enemies.

Q: What were the false teachers teaching?
A: The false teachers were not telling the truth about Jesus. They were teaching about a different "Jesus" and "Holy Spirit." They were saying there was a different way of salvation. The false teachers were good speakers, but what they were saying was untrue.

Q: What were the false teachers saying about Paul?
A: These false teachers were saying Paul was not a good speaker. They said he wrote "bold" letters, but was "timid" in person. The false teachers said he was weak, and they tried to lure the Christians away from listening to him.

Study Questions

- What does it mean when Paul speaks of a treasure held in earthen vessels? (4:7)
- What warnings did Paul give the Corinthian church? (13:1–10)

GALATIANS

The Apostle Paul wrote the Letter to the Galatians to help people understand that it is not rule-keeping that makes a person a Christian.

Paul had visited Galatia (now in Turkey). He preached the gospel to Gentiles, who put their faith in Jesus and became Christians.

Some other Christians said that faith in Jesus was not enough. They said that all Christians had to keep the Law of Moses in order to be saved. Paul's letter explained that trying to keep the Law of Moses did not save anybody—not even the Jews—because no one can keep the Law. Paul reminded the Galatians that it is only faith in Jesus that can save a person.

What was true for the Galatians is true for us, too: Jesus is the only Person who could keep the whole Law. By trusting in Jesus, we become good in God's eyes. This was good news for the Galatians—and it's good news for us as well.

OUTLINE

Two problems (1—2)
Paul writes to correct two wrong ideas. One is that people must obey the Jewish customs and laws to be children of God; the second is that Paul is not really an Apostle.

We are justified by faith (3—4)
Paul spends a good deal of time explaining to the Galatians that we become God's children through faith in Jesus, no matter how good we are or how many laws we follow.

We are free in Christ (5—6)
Because we are justified by faith, and not by our good deeds, we are free to be loved by God despite our transgressions.

Remains of the ancient city of Antioch in Pisidia, visited by Paul. The Apostle wrote his Letter to the Galatians to the Christians of Antioch and other nearby towns.

Remains of the ancient stadium in the city of Perga, visited by Paul during his missionary travels

Frequently Asked Questions

Q: What were the rules the Jews had to keep?

A: The Jews had many ceremonial laws about worship, food, work, and cleanliness. Paul said God used the Law like a schoolteacher to show people that they can't be good enough without Jesus.

Q: Did Jesus get rid of the Law?

A: Jesus said He did not come to destroy the Law, but to fulfill it. He is the only One Who is perfect and can do everything to please God the Father.

Q: Does this mean that Christians can do whatever they want?

A: Paul teaches that we have to live virtuous lives guided by the Holy Spirit of God.

Look out for...

As you read Galatians, look out for...

The Law. *Jews have a great many laws and customs. Paul says much about the Christian attitude to those laws and customs.*

Freedom. *Paul wants Christians to have freedom and joy in Christ. He mentions this quite a bit.*

Faith. *Paul explains faith in many of his letters, and especially in Galatians.*

Jewish religious teachers discuss the Hebrew Torah.

Judaizers

In the Old Testament, God promised Abraham that he would become the father of a great nation. That nation was the Jewish nation. They had many laws and customs and a special relationship with Him. God willed that the Messiah, Jesus, would come from that group of people.

When Jesus died on the Cross, He died for everyone's sin. After Jesus returned to heaven, some of the Apostles preached the Good News of salvation not only to the Jews, but also to the Gentiles. This greatly upset some people. They believed that a person had to become a Jew, or at least obey Jewish customs, to really be a child of God. These people were called Judaizers and were the main reason why Paul wrote his Letter to the Galatians.

Study Questions

- How should a person use the freedom Christ gives? (5:13–21)
- How should a Christian behave? (5:22–26)

EPHESIANS

The Apostle Paul was in jail for teaching and preaching about Jesus, but his letters were full of good news. The Letter to the Ephesians was written to teach and encourage the Christians in Ephesus and other churches nearby.

Ephesians is filled with praise to God for His gift of salvation. It talks about Jesus Christ as the Head of all Christians everywhere. Everyone who believes in Jesus is part of His Body, the Church. Another way to view this is that Christians are in a new family—God's family.

Paul described many of the benefits of belonging to God's family. He also explained to his readers how to live in ways that were pleasing to God. Ephesians has important information about the way people should behave within their families.

Paul knew the devil was real and that Christians were in a battle against him. He encouraged believers to use God's spiritual weapons to fight against the enemy. Today, people still read Ephesians both to be encouraged and to learn how to love and respect God.

OUTLINE

Greetings (1:1–2)
Paul usually says who he is, and to whom he is writing, at the beginning of his letters.

Beliefs of the Church (1:3—3:21)
Salvation comes from Jesus. Wisdom comes from God. We are alive in Christ and one in Him. We are Christ's Body.

God is going to transform the world through us.

Actions of the Church (4—6)
Paul talks about the importance of humility, gentleness, unity, truthfulness, respect, purity, godly homes, strong families, good workers, and strong people prepared for spiritual wars.

Ephesus in the Time of Paul

Ephesus was a rich port city in the Roman province of Asia. It boasted a famous temple to Artemis (top left) of which almost nothing now remains. During Paul's visit, there was a riotous meeting in the massive theater when many of the people objected to Paul's preaching. The city also boasted a stadium (near the theater) and an agora that served as a marketplace (the colonnaded square near the theater).

Look out for...

As you read Ephesians, look out for...

God's plan for us. *Ephesians tells us a great deal about how God wants us to be imitators of Him in our actions and behavior.*

Personal qualities. *Ephesians relates many qualities that we should show in our lives.*

The Church. *Paul tells the Ephesians about the Church and what God has planned for it.*

A Roman infantryman with his arms and protective clothing

Spiritual warfare

A spiritual war is a war against Satan and evil, not against another country or person. Ephesians 6:10–18 is one of the most famous passages about spiritual warfare. It tells us to be prepared, using different types of military protection to describe the tools we need to fight evil. Truth is described as a belt. The zeal for peace is described as shoes. Faith is described as a shield. Salvation is described as a helmet. The word of God is described as the sword of the Spirit. Prayer does not have a word picture, but it is mentioned as an important way to fight evil.

Frequently Asked Question

Q: What is the greatness in being in God's family?
A: A person who is in God's family is alive in Christ, has God's mercy and salvation, has Christ's power to obey God and to love others, and can call God "Father."

Study Questions

- How do good deeds help a person be saved? (2:8–10)
- What are some of the reasons why Christians should do good deeds? (4:20–24)
- What special advice does this letter have for children and parents? (6:1–4)

PHILIPPIANS

OUTLINE

Greetings and thanks (1:1–20)

Paul is very close to the people in the Philippian church. He thanks God for them.

Suffering for Christ (1:21–30)

Paul has suffered a great deal, including being in jail for his faith. Yet, he still believes in Christ's mercy and God's goodness.

Living the Christian life (2)

Paul writes about humility, thankfulness, and the examples of Timothy and Epaphroditus.

Knowing Christ (3)

Some people call this Paul's statement of faith. He says that the most important thing in life is knowing Christ and spending every day striving to know Him better.

Paul's goodbye (4)

Paul loves these people and takes time in thanking them. He also tells them to be strong and to rejoice.

Remains of the theater in Philippi, Macedonia

Paul wrote this letter to the church in Philippi. He wrote about his joy while in jail, even when people were against him. Paul knew that God had allowed him to be in jail so that the gospel could be preached there.

He wrote that to follow Christ's example and serve others brings real joy. Paul reminded the church in Philippi that Jesus is the only true source of joy. Compared with Jesus, everything else is worthless.

Paul's letter to the Christians in Philippi was also a note of thanks, for they had sent him a gift of money. Paul was heartened that the Christians wished to share his work. It was their love that gave him joy.

When you reach the low points in life, the Letter to the Philippians can give you a reason to be joyful.

Philippi

Philippi was a city in ancient Macedonia. Macedonia belonged to both the Romans and the Greeks. Its greatest leader was King Philip, father of Alexander the Great. Macedonia was the first part of Europe to hear the gospel, which Paul brought there. He meant a great deal to the Christians of Macedonia.

Philippi was an important city. Paul may have visited Philippi on his missionary journeys because so many roads went through it. If all of Macedonia was going to hear the gospel, Philippi was an ideal starting point.

An ancient Greek warrior

Remains of the ancient prison in Philippi, where Paul and Silas were jailed

Frequently Asked Questions

Q: Why were some people against Paul?
A: Some preachers were jealous of Paul. They thought they could make his life difficult by preaching, too. In truth, they also wanted to make a name for themselves. It buoyed Paul that the message of Jesus was being told—even if some people's motives were wrong.

Q: How did Paul preach the gospel if he was in jail?
A: Paul spoke to the Roman soldiers who were guarding him. These people, who probably would never have gone to hear him preach, heard him every day. Furthermore, other Christians grew brave when they witnessed Paul's courage in speaking up about Jesus.

Study Questions

- What are Christians supposed to think about and do? (4:8–9)
- How should Christians handle money? (4:11–13)

COLOSSIANS

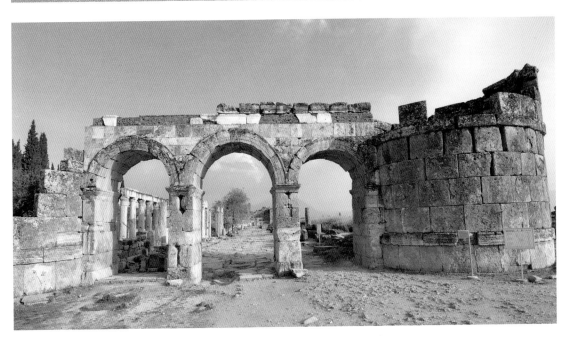

For some people, the gospel of Jesus Christ is just too simple. They want to make it complicated. They think there should be secret knowledge and special ceremonies in which a person must participate to be saved. The Apostle Paul wrote the Letter to the Colossians to eliminate such mistaken ideas.

False teachers were telling the Colossians that they had to eat and drink certain things and worship in special ways to be Christians. Paul, however, said that simply having faith in Jesus Christ is what makes a person a Christian.

The false teachers also taught that people needed to worship angels to reach God. Jesus is the only One we need to reach the Father. Today, many people are interested in angels. Angels are God's messengers—but we are not to worship them.

Additionally, the false teachers taught wrongly that the body is evil. They even said it doesn't matter what Christians do with their bodies. Paul explained that God created people's bodies and that Christians should use them in ways that are pure and holy.

Singing to God, living at peace with others, and doing everything to glorify Jesus Christ are some of the instructions Paul gave to the Colossian Christians. Such behavior is also important for believers today.

Gate to the ancient city of Hierapolis, Asia Minor, near the biblical city of Colossae

OUTLINE

Greetings and thanks (1:1–14)

Paul usually explains who he is at the beginning of the letter. Here he also gives some news, not unlike what is written in any letter today.

Christ is above everything else (1:15–29)

The Colossians need to understand that Christ is God, only Christ died for our sins, and only Christ is worthy of our worship.

What to believe (2)

Several false teachings are discussed. Some people worship angels. Some people impose too many harsh rules on themselves. Some people suffer from pride. Paul talks about each of these problems.

How to live in Christ (3:1—4:6)

This is the Good News. Paul points out that since Christ is above all and has forgiven our sins, we have wonderful lives to live. We also have a responsibility to make wise choices and to love one another.

Final goodbyes (4:7–18)

Paul finishes his letter much as any letter-writer would: he sends additional news and some instructions.

Frequently Asked Questions

Q: Why did Paul remind the Christians that Jesus is God?

A: False teachers were saying that the body is evil, so God would not have come in bodily form. Paul made it clear that Jesus was both God and Man at the same time.

Q: Why did the false teachers want people to have special ceremonies and rules?

A: The false teachers wanted their own religion to have such trappings because it made them feel important.

Look out for...

As you read Colossians, look out for...

Titles of Christ. Paul uses many different titles for Jesus, because Jesus does so many things in our lives and means so much to us.

Doctrines and beliefs. Paul is writing to correct some false teachings. Because of this, you will find much about different beliefs.

Instructions to families. Paul tells us some ways to be good family members.

Quayside scene at a Mediterranean port in Roman times. It is likely Paul would have sailed in a trading vessel of this kind.

Study Questions

- What instructions did Paul give for Christian living? (3:1–17)
- How are Christian families supposed to live? (3:18–21)

1 THESSALONIANS

Paul wrote two letters to the Christians at Thessalonica. This is a panel from a relief, picturing an offering at a pagan altar, from the Arch of Galerius in Thessalonica.

The church at Thessalonica was a young church. It began as a result of Paul's preaching during his second missionary journey. About two or three years later, he wrote the letter now called 1 Thessalonians.

Paul told the believers that he prayed for them often. He encouraged them to continue in their faith in Christ. He reminded them how he had lived and worked with them and how much he loved them. Paul said he was like a mother to the believers, and he missed them.

The city of Thessalonica was both significant and busy. Idol-worship was common there, and Christians were persecuted. Paul wanted to know whether the believers remained faithful to Christ, so in the midst of these circumstances

he sent his friend Timothy to encourage them. Paul was gladdened to learn they were still following the Lord.

One thing troubled the Christians of Thessalonica: they didn't understand why it was taking Jesus so long to return. Paul told them that no one except the Father knew when Jesus would return. His advice was that they should continue living holy lives that would be pleasing to God.

The Thessalonians also were concerned about the people they loved who had already died. Would those who had died miss Jesus' return? Paul told them that believers who died would be the first to rise and return with Jesus. The mission of those who remain on earth is to live pure and peaceful lives.

OUTLINE

The conversion of the Thessalonians (1)

When the Thessalonians came to believe in Christ, they followed Him wholeheartedly.

The beginning of the church in Thessalonica (2)

Paul shares his memories of when he and Silas helped start the church.

Paul's concern and instruction for the church (3:1—4:12)

Paul is concerned about the suffering the church there has endured.

Jesus' return (4:13—5:11)

Paul explains that Christians who have died will be raised to life when Jesus returns.

Paul's final instructions (5:12–28)

Paul reminds them to love each other and live for Christ.

Frequently Asked Questions

Q: Why didn't Paul go himself to see the Christians in Thessalonica?
A: Paul said that Satan stopped him from returning to Thessalonica (2:18). He doesn't explain what happened or how Satan prevented him from doing so.

Q: Who was Timothy?
A: Timothy was a fellow worker with Paul. He often accompanied Paul on his missionary journeys. Timothy sometimes carried letters from Paul to other believers.

Look out for...

As you read 1 Thessalonians, look out for...

Jesus' return. *Paul writes a great deal about this. Notice that chapters one to four all close with comments about the return of Christ.*

Paul's instructions. *Paul reminds the Thessalonians several times how they are to treat each other and live for Christ.*

The Second Coming

When Jesus came to earth to die for our sins, through the Incarnation, He took our human nature and became Man. The next time Jesus comes to earth, He will come as King to take us home to heaven. This is called the Second Coming.

The Thessalonians had many questions about the Second Coming. That's one of the main reasons Paul wrote this letter and 2 Thessalonians. We still are looking forward to the Second Coming. The Bible tells us frequently, including in the two Letters to the Thessalonians, to live holy lives so we can be ready to meet Christ face to face when He comes.

Study Question

• What encouragement did Paul give the Thessalonians about the Second Coming of Jesus? (4:13–18)

205

2 THESSALONIANS

Remains of the ancient Roman forum at Thessalonica, which Paul would have visited (Acts 17:1–9)

Some of the Christians in Thessalonica were confused about the Second Coming of Jesus. They misunderstood Paul's first letter to them; they thought Paul had told them Jesus' return was imminent. They decided to stop everything they were doing and just wait. Paul wrote the second Letter to the Thessalonians to help them understand what he actually meant.

Paul was glad they believed in Jesus, but he did not want them just to remain idle. He became aware that some people were not even working to provide for their families. Instead of being busy at work, they simply wasted time involved in others' business.

The advice Paul gave was strong. He said, "Anyone who was unwilling to work should not eat" (3:10). Paul said the believers should admonish those who were refusing to work.

OUTLINE

Greetings and thanks (1)
The Thessalonians stood strong during persecution and Paul commends them.

The Second Coming (2)
Paul tells the Thessalonians not to worry that the end has begun and relates signs of Jesus' coming.

Instructions and helpful words (3)
Paul encourages the church to keep busy by doing good.

Paul wanted the Christians to watch and work while waiting for Christ's return. This letter gives today's faithful good advice about how to live while waiting for Jesus' Second Coming—be faithful.

Look out for...

As you read 2 Thessalonians, look out for...

Signs of the Second Coming. *Particularly in chapter two, Paul explains these signs, so that we can be prepared.*

Persecution. *Some people were harassing Christians simply because they were Christians. Paul wrote encouraging words to these Christians.*

Frequently Asked Questions

Q: Why did the Thessalonians think Jesus was coming imminently?

A: Many Christians were in grave trouble with the government. Roman officials did not like Christians and were allowed to harass them, hurt them, and even kill them just for being Christians. Thus, the Thessalonian Christians thought that Jesus would be returning at any moment to rescue them.

Q: What should we do while waiting for Jesus to return?

A: We should do everything God has told us to do. We should work at our jobs, obey God, serve Him, take care of our families, tell others about Jesus, help the needy, pray faithfully, love others, build up the Church, and do good.

The antichrist

John mentions the antichrist in 1 and 2 John. There he is speaking about someone within his community who was opposed to Christ. In 2 Thessalonians 2:8, Paul talks about the "lawless one." In fact, ever since Old Testament days, God's people have known about a person or power at the end of time who will attack them. That attack will be crushed by Jesus, the Messiah.

Paul wanted the Christians in Thessalonica to understand that the antichrist had not come yet, so Christ's coming was not about to happen in the next days or weeks. He gave them this sign to look for so they would continue working until Christ came.

Study Question

• What did Paul say would happen before Jesus Christ returns? (2:1–12)

A Roman oil lamp, made of clay

1 TIMOTHY

When the Apostle Paul was older, he wrote to Timothy, a bishop, to give him advice. Because Paul wanted Timothy to do a good job leading the church at Ephesus, he wrote to him about what was important. His letter, called 1 Timothy, has good advice for church leaders and the faithful even today.

Paul said that doctrine—the guiding principles of the faith—is very important. He did not want Christians to become confused and believe lies about Jesus or about being a Christian. He told Timothy to pray for rulers who would allow Christians to live peaceful lives.

Born to a Jewish Christian mother and Greek father, Timothy became an important friend and helper to Paul.

Paul also said the life of the church is very important. He advised Timothy how believers should worship God and gave instructions about choosing church leaders. Churches are made up of people of all ages and in different circumstances. Paul advised Timothy how to treat people kindly, yet firmly. This letter is a good guide for any Christian learning to serve God and His people.

OUTLINE

Greetings and instruction (1)
Paul asks Timothy to stay at Ephesus and deal with the teachers who aren't doing what is right.

Instructions for worship (2)
Paul urges the people to pray and prepare for worship.

Instructions for church leaders (3)
Church leaders must live holy and respectable lives.

How to handle false teachers (4)
Timothy should take a stand against false teachers by teaching the truth.

How to treat each other (5:1—6:2)
Treat elders with respect and take care of widows.

Riches and a godly life (6:3–21)
People should concentrate more on loving God than on acquiring money.

Elders and deacons

Elders and deacons both served as church leaders in Timothy's day. Elders were presbyters and they seem to have had a council to guide the community. Some communities were led by bishops (literally, overseers). They were to have good reputations and live blameless lives. Their job in the church was to keep an eye on the spiritual growth of the community and the teaching of God's Word. Timothy performed this work admirably.

The first deacons took care of feeding the church, so the Apostles had more time to teach.

Look out for...

As you read 1 Timothy, look out for...

Worship guidelines. *Paul tells Timothy how to lead the church in worship.*

Advice and instructions. *Paul is a friend and teacher to Timothy, so he gives him a good deal of meaningful advice.*

Reasons. *Paul doesn't just tell Timothy what to do. He also tells him why he needs to do things a certain way.*

A view of the site of ancient Ephesus from the top of the huge amphitheater, which the Apostle Paul knew from his visit. In his time, the sea came as far as the green area at the far end of the marble roadway, where the quay was situated.

Frequently Asked Questions

Q: Why did Paul think he should advise Timothy?
A: Paul and Timothy were close friends. Paul thought of Timothy as a son, and Timothy helped Paul in his ministry. Paul knew that being a pastor is an important responsibility and wanted to encourage Timothy.

Q: Why is it important to pray for government leaders?
A: If government leaders do what is good, everyone benefits. Their sound and suitable laws make it easier for everyone to lead a peaceful life.

Study Questions

• What kind of people should be leaders in the church? (3:1–13)
• How did Paul say that Timothy should treat the various people in the church? (5:1–21)

2 TIMOTHY

Paul was imprisoned in Rome, but still he was able to write lengthy letters to churches and to his believing friends.

The Apostle Paul was in prison, waiting to be executed for his faith in Christ. Paul wrote his last letter, which appears in the Bible as 2 Timothy, to the man he loved like a son. He wrote to Timothy to remind him how to be a good pastor.

Paul encouraged Timothy to remain true to his teachings about Christ and to pass on to other faithful Christians the Good News about Jesus. They then could teach others. This is precisely how we have received the message of Christ down through the ages.

One of the main things Paul told Timothy to teach was that Jesus was both wholly God and wholly Man. Paul warned that many people would not want to hear the truth—but Timothy was to continue teaching God's truth anyway.

OUTLINE

Be faithful (1)
Paul tells Timothy to live his life by the good teaching he has received. We need to do the same thing.

Be a good soldier (2)
Work hard for Christ, being faithful during hard times and staying away from needless arguments.

The last days (3:1–9)
Be ready for difficult times. Some things will get worse as the world continues to exist.

Paul's goodbye (3:10—4:22)
Paul tells Timothy to be strong for God. He also shares with him some news and sends greetings to friends. He concludes by asking Timothy to visit him soon.

In this letter, Paul also showed his great love for the Bible. He reinforced to Timothy that the Bible was inspired by God and is thus the perfect guidebook to show Christians how to live a Christian life. Paul asked Timothy to visit him in prison and bring his "papers" to him. These were probably copies of Old Testament books. It was through reading and knowing God's Word that Paul built up his faith in Christ.

Paul's imprisonment

Paul wrote this letter when he was in prison, waiting to be executed. His only crime was telling others about Jesus. He had been under arrest once before, but he had been released. This time, he had no reason to believe he would be freed.

Paul didn't have many visitors because people were afraid to come to see him. Thus, Paul was alone in prison, probably in chains, waiting to die. Yet, neither depression nor self-pity overtook him. He wrote to Timothy so that he could continue the work that Paul had begun.

This is what makes this letter special: Paul told Timothy the things that were most important to him because he knew that it might be one of his last chances to do so. Paul wrote so that Timothy would be strong. We can read this letter and gain strength as well.

Look out for…

As you read 2 Timothy, look out for…

Advice. Paul writes this letter to give Timothy important advice. It's good advice for us, too.

Difficult times. Paul has been through some rough times: jail, beatings, huge disappointments, and now prison. He tries to prepare Timothy for similar troubles.

People. Paul mentions twenty-seven different people in this letter. This is more than in any of his other letters.

Study Questions

- What did Paul say people will be like in the last days? (3:1–5)
- How did Paul describe the Bible? (3:16)
- How did Paul face his coming death? (4:6–8)

Frequently Asked Questions

Q: What proof did Paul give that Jesus was both God and Man?
A: Paul reminded Timothy that Jesus rose from the dead and was descended from King David.

Q: Why didn't Paul have his papers with him in prison?
A: Paul was probably arrested and taken to prison hurriedly and was unable to take his things with him.

TITUS

Paul was facing execution because of his faith in Jesus. Titus was a Greek believer who had journeyed with Paul on some of his missionary journeys. When Paul needed a strong leader for the churches on the island of Crete, he sent Titus. He told Titus to help the believers build a strong church.

The letter Paul wrote to Titus bears his name, Titus. It is the third letter to a pastor (the others are 1 Timothy and 2 Timothy).

Titus also needed help in serving the church. Paul gave him advice about what sort of people should be leaders. He made it clear that church leaders have to be people who study God's Word, and they also must follow Jesus. Titus would have to be on his guard against false teachers.

Paul gave Titus other instructions, too. He told Titus how the believers should live. Paul stressed that once a person becomes a follower of Christ, he or she should want to do what is right and pleasing to God.

Titus was a Gentile Christian and friend and helper of Paul.

OUTLINE

Church leaders (1:1–9)
Church leaders should be loving people who consider God in everything they do.

False teachers (1:10–16)
Church leaders should warn their people about false teaching.

Right living in the church (2)
We need to teach each other and do what is right.

Right living in society (3)
When we obey the law of the land, we help others see God living through us.

Frequently Asked Questions

Q: **Why did the churches on Crete need strong leaders?**
A: The people of Crete had a reputation of being lazy and undisciplined. The Christians there needed encouragement to live their lives more faithfully. This would make them good examples of how God can change people.

Q: **Are there any other letters to church leaders like Titus?**
A: The first and second Letters to Timothy are also letters to a church leader.

Balos beach, Crete

Crete

Crete is an island just south of Greece. When Paul was alive, it was a large and properous island with almost one hundred cities. He and his friends had started churches in many of those cities. When Paul left, however, someone was needed to help people in those cities grow as Christians.

Paul tells Titus that the people of Crete were described as liars, lazy, and cruel. Titus had a demanding job helping the people of Crete to follow God and obey Him, rather than live the way most Cretans did. Since Titus had worked with difficult people before, perhaps this is why Paul sent him to this troubled place.

Look out for...

As you read Titus, look out for...

Christian leaders. *Paul wrote to Titus to describe the qualities a Christian leader needed.*

Grace and salvation. *Paul says we should live godly lives to gain God's grace and salvation.*

Study Questions

- What should church leaders be like? (1:6–9)
- What were the false teachers like? (1:10–16)
- How should Christians live? (2:1–15)

PHILEMON

Onesimus the slave presents his master, Philemon, with Paul's letter.

Philemon was probably a rich Christian: the church met in his home and he had slaves. Paul wrote to ask Philemon to forgive his runaway slave, Onesimus. Onesimus had fled to Rome and had at some point met Paul and become a Christian.

Paul told Philemon he prayed for him and thanked God for Philemon's love for believers. Paul then told Philemon that his slave Onesimus had become a believer. Paul asked him to accept Onesimus back as a brother, appealing to Philemon's love for him.

Look out for...

As you read Philemon, look out for...

Reasons. Paul gives Philemon various reasons for showing kindness to Onesimus.

Study Question

• How did Paul think Philemon would respond to his request? (verse 21)

A troop of men in Roman military costume

Slaves

Slaves were common in the Roman world of Paul's time. Some people sold themselves into slavery to pay off debts. A number of these people were treated more like servants than slaves. Many young girls were sold to be maids and to take care of a household or of children.

Laws governed the treatment of slaves, but some slaves were still badly treated because they were regarded as property. Paul didn't try to abolish slavery; instead, he pointed out that God made us all and that we should love everyone, no matter who they are.

A Roman slave badge

Frequently Asked Questions

Q: Why did the church meet in Philemon's house?
A: The people didn't have a church building, so they met in Philemon's house. It was common for the early churches to gather in private houses like his.

Q: Why did Philemon have a slave?
A: Slavery was common at this time. Paul asked Philemon to receive Onesimus back as a brother rather than a slave.

HEBREWS

Hebrews was written to Jewish Christians who were wondering if it might be better to return to their former Jewish faith. They were first-century Christians who may have been puzzled why Jesus had not returned yet to set up His Kingdom.

The writer of Hebrews makes it clear that everything about Jesus Christ is better than any other leader or religion. Jesus is superior to the prophets, angels, Moses, the Jewish priests, and the whole Old Testament way of serving God. Jesus is better because He is God.

The inspired author of Hebrews (for centuries, it was thought to be Paul, though this is now disputed) said that the people should have been mature Christians by the time he wrote the letter, but that they were still like babies needing milk. He encouraged them to do good, so they would be strong and able to resist when tempted.

Hebrews is probably best known for chapter 11. Many believers of the past are listed in this Hall of Faith. For some 2,000 years, it has encouraged Christians to trust in God.

Christians today can read the Letter to the Hebrews and be reminded to stay true to Christ because He is the best Gift of God the Father.

OUTLINE

Christ is above everything else (1:1—4:13)
Christ is greater than the angels and greater than Moses.

Jesus as priest (4:14—10:18)
Jesus is the greatest high priest who has ever lived and ever will live.

Christians must endure (10:19—12:29)
Examples of people who believed in God. People are encouraged to hold on to their faith, no matter what.

Goodbyes and personal notes (13:1–25)
The writer encourages believers to live obedient lives.

Look out for...

As you read Hebrews, look out for...

Faith facts. *Hebrews talks a good deal about people with faith and how God responds to their faith.*

Characteristics of Jesus. *Hebrews talks about Jesus' many different roles, including those of prophet and priest.*

God's love. *Hebrews reminds us that God loves and cares for us.*

Frequently Asked Questions

Q: Why would Jewish Christians want to give up their faith in Jesus?

A: Oftentimes, people think fondly of the past. That is what these Jewish Christians were doing. They remembered the old ways and wondered if they were all right after all. God had revealed Himself to the Jewish (Hebrew) people in the Old Testament; they were special to Him. The Jewish Christians were forgetting, however, that Jesus is more important than anything else.

Q: How does Hebrews say that Jesus is best?

A: Hebrews reminds us that angels are God's messengers, but Jesus is God's Son. Prophets told about the Messiah coming, but Jesus is the Messiah. Priests had to sacrifice daily for sin, but Jesus sacrificed Himself once for all sin.

Herod's Temple, covered in white marble and decorated in gold, glittered in the bright sunlight of Jerusalem.

Faith

Hebrews connects the Old Testament to the New Testament through faith in Christ. The writer of Hebrews gives many examples of people in the Old Testament who believed in Jesus even before He came to earth. They believed because they read in the Old Testament that Christ was coming. They were saved by trusting in God, just as people are saved today because of the merits of Jesus' death and Resurrection.

Hebrews also encourages us to have faith. As you read the New Testament, and especially Hebrews, you can look back on Christ's life, just as the Old Testament believers looked forward to Christ's life. It is faith in Christ that ties the whole Bible together.

Study Questions

- How was Jesus a high priest? (9:11–14)
- What did God do for the people in the Old Testament who stayed faithful to Him? How do we have a part in His promises? (11:1–40)

JAMES

We don't naturally thank God for trouble. Usually, we do whatever we can to avoid it. But the Letter of James starts with advice to let trouble be an opportunity for joy (1:2).

The people to whom James was writing were Jewish Christians living among Gentiles. Many of them suffered for being Christians. Non-Christians would harass and mock them for their faith. James told his readers that these troubles could teach them to grow strong in Christ. It is for that reason that he said they should be thankful for their problems.

The Letter of James teaches that faith is shown by actions. A person shouldn't just declare that he or she is a Christian, but also should live like one. A Christian should want to live the way Jesus taught people should live. After all, God loves us so much He sent Jesus to die for us.

James wrote that our words reflect what we are like. It is important to ask God for wisdom, for He will help us to know how to speak to others.

The Letter to James also teaches that we should not let a person's riches or poverty affect our attitude to him or her. We should be kind to all people equally.

James teaches that faith and actions are both important to God.

OUTLINE

James' greetings (1:1)
James was writing to Jewish Christians everywhere.

Endurance (1:2–18)
When life is difficult, faith should grow stronger, rather than weaker.

Hearing and doing the Word of God (1:19—2:26)
If we truly believe what God says, we will act upon it.

Our words and God's wisdom (3)
The words we speak can have very positive—or very negative—effects. We need God's wisdom to control our words.

Trusting God (4)
We never know what will happen next, but we always can trust all things to God.

General advice on Christian living (5)
Do not trust money more than God. Trust Him when life is difficult. Keep praying and showing love.

James, the author of this letter, is usually thought to be James, the brother, that is relative, of Jesus.

The busy Damascus Gate gives entry to the Old City of Jerusalem.

A Jewish high priest in his special dress. At the Jerusalem Temple, certain sacrifices had to be offered by the high priest, and he alone could enter the Holiest Place.

Look out for...

As you read James, look out for...

Direct instructions. *James does not play games: he tells Christians exactly what they must do to follow God.*

Evidence of faith. *James tells us how to find out if our faith is true faith—by being mindful of how we live.*

Words. *How we use our words shows a great deal about our faith.*

Frequently Asked Questions

Q: Does joy mean a person is laughing and singing when something really bad happens?

A: Joy is not the same as happiness. Happiness is usually the result of a good experience, a fun-filled time. Joy is deeper: it is a peace we have because we know God is in control and with us—no matter what happens.

Q: How can a person show faith?

A: No one can live a perfect Christian life, but a person who has faith in Jesus should be trying to live the way God told us to live. A Christian should read God's Word and ask the Holy Spirit for help to do God's will.

Oaths

When someone takes an oath, that person calls on God as a witness. The person is saying that God Himself would say the same thing because it is true. In Bible times, oaths were taken very seriously. There were simple oaths for everyday use and solemn oaths for important occasions. When swearing an oath, someone might raise his or her hand and say, "as sure as the Lord who rescues Israel lives."

An everyday oath today would be saying, "Cross my heart and hope to die." A more solemn oath would be that taken when people testify in court. They raise their right hand and put their left hand on the Bible, if one is used, and swear or promise to tell "the truth, the whole truth, and nothing but the truth."

James (and Jesus) said we should not take oaths. We should be truthful people, so that our "yes" means "yes" and our "no" means "no." We should have a reputation for being so honest that no one needs an oath to believe us.

Model of Herod's Temple, Jerusalem. James was leader of the believers in Jerusalem. This Temple was destroyed by the Romans in A.D. 70.

Study Questions

- How can difficult times and problems be good? (1:2–4)
- Why is it important for us to watch what we say? (3:3–12)

1 PETER

Peter wrote this letter to Christians who, because of their faith, were being persecuted, tortured, and even threatened with their lives. He wrote it to encourage them. They were scattered throughout Asia Minor (in modern-day Turkey) and were under pressure for believing in Jesus. Some Christians here had already been killed for their faith in Christ.

Peter spoke from experience. He himself had been beaten and put in prison because he preached about Jesus. He drew comfort from God's love in giving him eternal life. Peter also knew that being persecuted for his faith strengthened it. God had promised His children eternal life with Him in heaven, and that applied to him and to all his Christian readers. He thus told them to expect trouble and not to fear it.

This letter was written a long time ago, but many Christians still suffer persecution and ridicule today. Believers in Jesus can learn from Peter how to accept such suffering and look forward to life with Christ in heaven.

OUTLINE

Peter's greetings (1:1–2)
Peter explains who he is and to whom he is writing.

Salvation (1:3—2:3)
God provided a way of salvation through Jesus. Because we have received that salvation, we should live holy lives.

Do what's right (2:4—3:12)
Because we're Christians, we have a responsibility to do what is right. This means we should be true in our relationships.

Suffering (3:13—4:19)
Sometimes we suffer for doing what is right. Even when we are suffering, we still have a responsibility to obey God.

Final advice (5)
Peter tells the leaders of the church to be wise and strong.

Peter began his working life as a fisherman, until he was called by Jesus to become a fisher of men.

Persecution

Persecution—oppressing, harassing, or making someone's life extremely difficult in any way possible—was common during Peter's life. At that time, the Roman emperor Nero was persecuting Christians in Rome.

The persecution happened in many different ways. Sometimes Nero had Christians beaten or put in jail, and sometimes he had them killed. It is likely you have heard stories about Christians being put into an arena with lions. Throughout history, governments and people have hated Christians and hated God. For this reason, Christians have sometimes been persecuted; yet, through encouragement such as Peter gives, many have stood strong.

The Colosseum, Rome, by night. While it has been thought that many Christians faced death in this arena because of their faith, it seems that many more were put to death in the horse racing site, the Circus Maximus.

Look out for...

As you read 1 Peter, look out for...

***Obeying authority.** Peter talks about authority in the Church as well as in the city or nation.*

***What Christ has done for us.** In many different ways, Peter tells us what Christ has done for us.*

***Suffering.** Christians are being persecuted. This is why it is important for Peter to write about suffering.*

Frequently Asked Questions

Q: What good is it if Christians are persecuted for their faith?
A: If Christians live godly lives, their enemies may accuse them of doing evil, but, in the end, they will bring glory to God.

Q: Why should Christians expect suffering?
A: Christians are followers of Jesus. If He suffered, His followers will suffer as well. Many people do not want to be told that Jesus is the only way to God.

Study Questions

- How can Christians grow and mature? (2:1–3)
- How should Christians treat people in authority? (2:13–17)
- What should Christians do about Satan? (5:8–9)

2 PETER

Peter is arrested for belonging to the Church (Acts 12:1–19).

The Apostle Peter wrote this second letter to urge Christians to stay close to God. Peter knew he would soon be killed for his beliefs, and he wanted to encourage Christians to continue to grow in their faith in Christ.

He told them how important it was to know the Scriptures and to know Christ better and better. Peter pointed out that the Bible is God's Word and is not invented by the people who wrote it down.

Peter also warned against false teachers who would come into the Church after he had gone. He said they would deceive people and lead them into sin, and Peter did not want that to happen

to his brothers and sisters in Christ. Also, there would be those who denied that Jesus was coming a second time. Peter wanted believers to know that Jesus was delaying His return because God was patient and was giving people time to repent. Meanwhile, Christians should live blameless lives in peace with God and share the gospel with those around them.

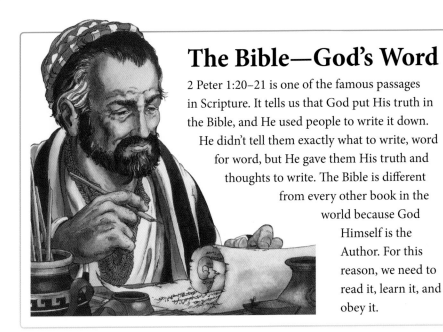

The Bible—God's Word

2 Peter 1:20–21 is one of the famous passages in Scripture. It tells us that God put His truth in the Bible, and He used people to write it down. He didn't tell them exactly what to write, word for word, but He gave them His truth and thoughts to write. The Bible is different from every other book in the world because God Himself is the Author. For this reason, we need to read it, learn it, and obey it.

Frequently Asked Questions

Q: What kind of things would false teachers teach?

A: Peter warned that people calling themselves Christians would deny Jesus was Lord. They would blaspheme, live immoral lives, tell others that immorality is acceptable, and boast.

Q: Why did Peter write about the destruction of the world?

A: False teachers were denying Jesus' Second Coming. Peter wanted Christians to know that they were wrong. He wrote that one day, Jesus would return and God would create a new home for all His people.

Look out for...

As you read 2 Peter, look out for...

The ingredients of spiritual growth.
It does not happen without effort.

Characteristics of false teachers.
Notice how God will treat them.

Study Questions

- Where did Scripture come from? (1:20–21)
- How does God see time? (3:8–9)
- Since God is going to judge us, how should Christians live? (3:11–13)

1 JOHN

Darkness fell over Jerusalem when Jesus died on the Cross. John was an eyewitness of Jesus' life and death.

The Apostle John was an eyewitness to the life of Jesus. He had been there when Jesus was living on earth. He had heard Jesus with his own ears. He had seen Jesus with his own eyes. John knew Jesus personally. He knew all about Jesus and the truth about Jesus.

John wrote this letter because some people were teaching that Jesus was not really God in human form. They said Jesus was more like a ghost than a real human being. They also said that it did not matter what people did with their bodies since they would die anyway. These ideas were making Christians wonder if it was acceptable to sin.

John wanted Christians to know that Jesus is real and really gave them eternal life. He wanted them to know that anyone born into God's family does not sin as a way of life—but, when Christians do sin, they can ask Jesus to forgive them. He forgives people when they repent, and they can renew friendship with God and with each other. That is the truth about Jesus.

Remains of the Basilica of St. John, Ephesus. John likely left Jerusalem and spent his last years in the city of Ephesus.

Frequently Asked Questions

Q: How did John know that Jesus was God as well as a human being?

A: John was with Peter and James when Jesus was transfigured. They saw Jesus' divine glory. They also heard God the Father say that Jesus was His Son.

Q: How did John say people should love fellow humans?

A: John said that love is not just words but also actions. He said that if a Christian friend needs food or clothing, it is not enough to say, "I hope you find food or clothing." You need to provide the person with food or clothing. Christian love gives help to people in need.

Look out for...

As you read 1 John, look out for...

Love. *John's love for his readers, God's love for us, and our love for each other.*

Sin. *Its presence and what it causes in our lives.*

Study Questions

- What should a Christian do when he or she sins? (1:9)
- What does "love the world" mean? (2:15–17)
- What does John say Christians will be like when Jesus returns? (3:1–3)

2 JOHN

The shortest book in the Bible can be summed up in two words: truth and love.

The Apostle John wrote this short letter called 2 John. He warned the local church, his dear friends in Christ, to beware of those who were not teaching the truth. This faith community probably opened itself to journeying preachers, showing Christian love and hospitality. John warned that not all the teachers and preachers were telling the truth.

There were those who taught that Jesus was not really a human being; they denied the truth of Jesus Christ as God and Man. Their teaching was wrong. If the local church welcomed them, however, others would think the teachers were wise and listen to them. This would result in many becoming confused.

If people believe in a Jesus who is not the true Jesus, then they are not really trusting God.

Frequently Asked Question

Q: Why is it important that Jesus is God and Man?

A: Two reasons: first, only God is all good and therefore able to pay the debt for our sin; second, He needed to be human, so He could show us how to live in God's family here on earth. Jesus is a bridge between us and the heavenly Father.

OUTLINE

Greetings (verses 1–3)
John greets a Lady; this means a local church.

Remain faithful (verses 4–6)
Continue to love each other.

Beware of false teachers (verses 7–13)
Be careful about people who teach lies.

Look out for...

As you read 2 John, look out for...

Love. John always encourages his readers to love one another.

Strong warnings. John is outspoken when he talks about false teachers.

Study Questions

- What is God's definition of love? (verse 6)
- Why is 2 John so short? (verse 12)

3 JOHN

Journeying teachers and missionaries stayed in the homes of other Christians. One of those Christians was John's friend Gaius. The Apostle John wrote this short letter to him.

John was glad to know that Gaius was staying faithful to Christ, sharing his home and belongings with these preachers. It was important to John that Christians helped their fellow Christians. John did not want the missionaries to be in need.

Another man in the Church named Diotrephes was refusing to help the missionaries. He would not let others help them either. John instructed Gaius not to follow Diotrephes's bad example.

Frequently Asked Question

Q: Why didn't John want the nonbelievers to help the missionaries?
A: John did not want nonbelievers to think the missionaries and Christian teachers were just trying to get money for themselves.

Study Questions

- How did John show that our bodies and our spirits are important to God? (verse 2)
- What gave John joy? (verse 4)

OUTLINE

Greetings (verses 1–2)
From John to Gaius.

Good job! (verses 3–8)
Gaius has been very hospitable to journeying preachers.

Diotrephes (verses 9–10)
Diotrephes was making false charges against the Apostles and causing trouble in the Church.

Choose good examples (verses 11–15)
Demetrius is trustworthy and a good example for Gaius to follow.

Look out for...

As you read 3 John, look out for...

Hospitality. John compliments Gaius for looking after journeying preachers and missionaries.

JUDE

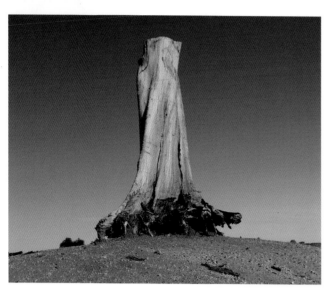

Jude warns that false teachers are like "trees in autumn barren and uprooted and so twice dead" (verse 12, NCV).

Ever since the beginning of the Church, Christians have had to beware of false teachers. Jude wrote this letter to warn believers that false teaching could lead to unfortunate results.

Jude was a brother of James and a relative of Jesus. Like James, at first he did not believe Jesus was the Messiah. After Jesus rose from the dead, however, Jude believed.

Jude's main concern was false teachers. They were saying Christians could do whatever they wanted because of God's freely given love. They said Christians did not have to obey any authority.

Opposing such teachings, Jude reminded Christians to stay close to Christ and to love and obey Him. He also said they should help others understand God's truth, so they could be saved as well.

Jude's purpose was not to frighten anyone. In fact, he closed his letter with the great promise that Jesus is able to keep us from falling. He praised Jesus for His majesty, power, and authority.

Frequently Asked Question

Q: Doesn't the Bible teach that God will forgive any sin?
A: God does forgive any sin for which there is true repentance. He, however, does not want people to live in sin. God wants us to turn to Him and trust in Jesus Christ. Then He gives us power to turn from our sin.

Sodom and Gomorrah

Jude refers to an Old Testament story about two towns, Sodom and Gomorrah (Genesis 18—19). God told Abraham He was going to destroy these towns because of their wickedness. Abraham's nephew, Lot, lived there, so Abraham asked God to spare the cities if he could find just ten righteous people there—but he could not find even ten.

God told Lot's family not to look back as they left. The town burned to the ground. Unfortunately, Lot's wife disobeyed God and looked back at her burning home—and turned into a pillar of salt.

To this day, as in Jude's day, Sodom and Gomorrah remind us that God judges sin.

Look out for...

As you read Jude, look out for...

Punishment of sin. *Jude spends much time telling us about sinful people and how God punished them.*

Christian life. *Jude closes with a solid description of the Christian life.*

Study Question

- How will it be when we see the Lord? (verses 24–25)

A rabbi holds up the precious Torah scroll in the synagogue.

REVELATION

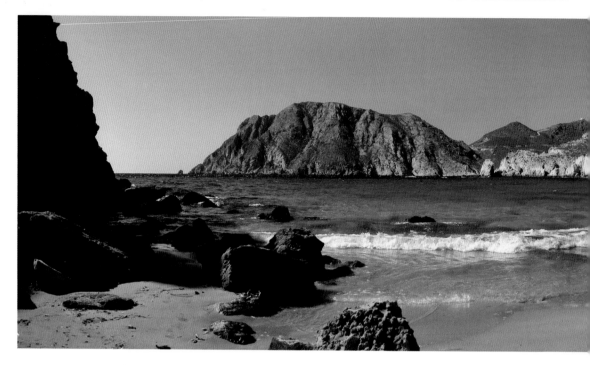

The Book of Revelation is also known as the Apocalypse. It includes promises of blessing to those who read, hear, and keep the words of Revelation.

The Apostle John wrote Revelation when he was very old. He was exiled on the island of Patmos because he refused to stop preaching about Jesus. Jesus gave John this vision to help Christians understand what was happening to them and what would happen in the future. Jesus gave special messages to seven different churches in Asia. Jesus commended the churches for their strengths and criticized them for their failings. He then told them how to correct their problems. These same problems exist today. Christians can learn from Jesus' words to these churches.

The Book of Revelation is filled with descriptive language. It tells how unbelievers will fight against Jesus and against God's people. It urges believers to stay true to Jesus and not to believe Satan's lies. In the end, it tells of Christ's great victory.

The joy of being with Jesus in heaven for all eternity far outweighs the difficulties we will have on earth.

The Book of Revelation does not so much tell people when the end of the world will happen as give them instruction on what to do in the meantime: give witness to the gospel.

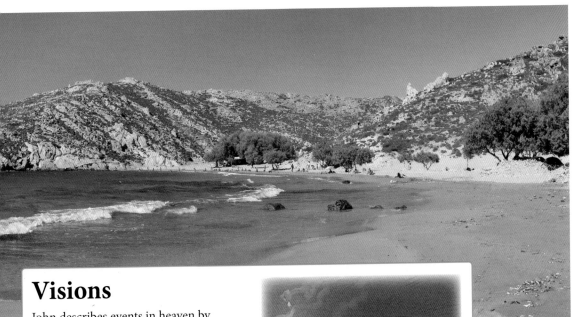

Visions

John describes events in heaven by comparing them with things we have seen on earth. These are his visions. Many visions are mentioned in the Bible. Jacob saw a vision of angels going up and down stairs that led to heaven (Genesis 28:10–15). Ezekiel saw many visions. In the first chapter of his book, he describes a vision of a windstorm and creatures that looked like men with wings and with feet like calves (Ezekiel 1:4–28). Daniel likewise had many visions. Some of Ezekiel's and Daniel's visions had to do with the last days of the earth, just as John's did.

Revelation describes many visions, including those of horses and riders. The book's many visions remind us that in spite of the difficult times that we might face for being Christians, we should give courageous witness to our faith.

A beach on the small Greek island of Patmos, where John was in exile

Seven Churches of Asia

AEGEAN SEA

MEDITERRANEAN SEA

Pergamum
Thyatira
Sardis
Philadelphia
Smyrna
Ephesus
Laodicea
Patmos

N

0   250 km
0   100 miles

Frequently Asked Questions

Q: What were the things for which Jesus commended the churches?
A: Jesus commended the churches for hard work, for suffering persecution and poverty, for being true to the faith, for love and service, and for being effective.

Q: What things were they doing that He did not like?
A: Jesus criticized the churches for forgetting their first love, for compromise, for immorality, for being superficial, and for being lukewarm. The churches at Smyrna and Philadelphia, however, got nothing but praise from Jesus.

OUTLINE

Jesus is coming back (1)
John describes his vision of Jesus returning.

Seven letters to seven churches (2—3)
John writes to seven churches, telling them positive things and negative things about the way they are serving God.

Vision of the end of earth as it is now (4—19)
John's visions include scrolls, trumpets, creatures we have never seen, angels, plagues, a wedding banquet, and horses.

The end of time (20—22)
John describes Satan's final punishment, the new earth and the new heaven.

Remains of the city of Laodicea, one of the places that John wrote a letter to, included in the Book of Revelation

Look out for...

As you read Revelation, look out for...

Messages to the churches. *There are seven messages for seven specific churches.*

Signs of the times. *John gives us many clues about what will happen when Christ returns and establishes His new Kingdom.*

Study Questions

- Who are the twenty-four elders and the four living creatures? (4:6-10)
- Who is the lady giving birth to the child, Mary or the Church? (12:1-6)
- What dreadful punishment awaits those who worship the beast? (14:9–11)
- What will eternity with God be like? (21:1—22:7)

Key Ideas in the Bible

Ascension: Jesus' return to heaven after His death and Resurrection.

Atonement: Payment for sin. Jesus' death atoned for all our sins.

Baptism: The sacrament that gives our souls the new life of sanctifying grace by which we become children of God and heirs of heaven. Baptism is called the "gateway of the sacraments," because unless we pass through this gateway, it is impossible to receive any of the other sacraments.

Beatitudes: A word meaning "blessings." Part of Jesus' Sermon on the Mount describes what makes people blessed.

Birthright: The legal right to be the leader of the family and to get a double amount of the inheritance when the father dies. Jacob traded a bowl of stew for the birthright of his brother, Esau.

The Sea of Galilee viewed from near the "Mount of Beatitudes"

Bless: To pray God's best for someone; to wish the person well; to speak well of the person.

Book of Life: The record of those who trust in Christ and will live in heaven with Him.

Born again: To be born spiritually by trusting in Christ's death and Resurrection.

Confess: To admit your sins; to say publicly what you believe.

Covenant: A promise or agreement between two or more people. God made a covenant with Abraham. God promised to bless the whole world through Abraham's descendants.

Cross: That on which the Romans executed Jesus; a symbol of Jesus' great love in taking away our sins.

Dedicate: To set something aside for God. Hannah dedicated Samuel to God before he was born.

Eternal life: The new life Jesus gives people when they trust in Him. Eternal life begins immediately and continues through eternity.

Faith: Complete trust in God that He exists and that what He says in the Bible is true. Obeying God.

Forgive: To pardon or cancel a debt; to wipe the record clean. When people place their trust in Jesus, God forgives their sin.

Fruits of the Spirit: The effects in us of the gifts of the Holy Spirit. The fruits are love, joy, peace, patience, kindness, generosity, faithfulness, gentleness, and self-control (Galatians 5:22–23).

Glorified: The state of those bodies when taken to heaven; the same as that of Jesus Himself (1 John 3:2–3).

Grace: God's free gift of the divine life of our soul.

Holiness: The state of sanctifying grace.

Justification: Being at peace with God. We are justified when we have faith, trusting in the promises that God has made to us through Jesus Christ.

Mercy: God's goodness to us, even though we do not deserve it.

Redemption: The work that Jesus did on the Cross: He paid the debt for our sin.

Repentance: Turning away from sin to God.

Resurrection: Rising from the dead. Jesus rose three days after He was crucified. Believers who die before Jesus returns will be resurrected at His Second Coming.

Salvation: The attainment of God in heaven through the freeing of the soul from sin and punishment.

Sin: Not cooperating with God's will; disobeying God; doing wrong. Every person sins.

Palm crosses, often distributed at Easter to remind believers of Palm Sunday and Good Friday

Soul: The spiritual part of a person; the source of one's life.

Temptation: Being drawn to what is wrong, to sin.

Unbelief: Refusing to believe in God or His Word; the opposite of faith.

Promises in the Bible

Promises made to believers

A rainbow, reminding us of God's promise to Noah

■ **A crown of life**
Revelation 2:10

■ **Answered prayer**
1 John 5:15

■ **A place in heaven**
John 14:1–3

■ **Cleansing**
John 15:3

■ **Comfort**
Isaiah 51:3

■ **Confidence for the future**
2 Timothy 1:12

■ **Eternal life**
John 3:16

■ **Gifts of the Spirit**
1 Corinthians 12

■ **God's guidance**
Isaiah 42:16

■ **Grace to the humble**
1 Peter 5:6–7

■ **Growth in the Christian life**
Ephesians 4:11–15

■ **Hope**
Hebrews 6:18–19

■ **Joy**
Isaiah 35:10

■ **Life in abundance**
John 10:10

■ **Peace**
John 14:27

■ **Rescue by God**
2 Timothy 4:18

■ **Rest**
Hebrews 4:9, 11

■ **Resurrection**
Romans 8:11

■ **Spiritual light**
John 12:46

■ **Strength**
Philippians 4:13

■ **Understanding**
Psalm 111:10

■ **Victory**
1 John 5:4

■ **Wisdom**
James 1:5

Fifty Very Important Passages

50 PASSAGES

The Bible is a lengthy book. Here are some of its most important passages.

Creation
Genesis 1, 2

The first sin
Genesis 3

Noah and the flood
Genesis 6—9:17

The tower of Babel
Genesis 11:1–9

Abraham and Isaac
Genesis 22:1–19

Esau and Jacob
Genesis 25:19–34; 27

The story of Joseph
Genesis 37—50

Baby Moses
Exodus 2:1–10

The Exodus
Exodus 7—14

The Ten Commandments
Exodus 20

Jericho is captured
Joshua 6:15–21

Gideon's little army
Judges 7:15–23

The story of Samson
Judges 13—16

The story of Ruth
Book of Ruth

The boy Samuel
1 Samuel 1—3

David kills Goliath
1 Samuel 17

The Good Shepherd psalm
Psalm 23

The fiery furnace
Daniel 3

Daniel in the lions' den
Daniel 6

The story of Jonah
Book of Jonah

The birth of Jesus
Luke 2

John the Baptist preaches
Matthew 3:1–12

Young Jesus in the Temple
Luke 2:41–52

The Baptism of Jesus
Matthew 3:13–17; Mark 1:9–11; Luke 3:21–22; John 1:31–34

Jesus is tempted
Matthew 4:1–11; Mark 1:12–13; Luke 4:1–13

The Sermon on the Mount
Matthew 5—7

The Lord's Prayer
Matthew 6:9–13; Luke 11:2–4

The woman at the well
John 4:1–30; 39–42

Becoming fishers of men
Matthew 4:18–22; Luke 5:1–11

A centurion's faith
Matthew 8:5–13; Luke 7:1–10

The story of the sower
Matthew 13:3–8, 18–23; Mark 4:3–8, 13–20; Luke 8:5–8, 11–15

The true vine
John 15

The prodigal son
Luke 15:11–32

Jesus is transfigured
Matthew 17:1–13; Mark 9:2–13; Luke 9:28–36

Mary and Martha
Luke 10:38–42

Zacchaeus
Luke 19:1–10

The anointing at Bethany
Matthew 26:6–13; Mark 14:3–9; John 12:1–8

The Last Supper
Matthew 26:17–30; Mark 14:12–26; Luke 22: 7–23

Jesus is betrayed
Matthew 26:14–16; Mark 14:10–11; Luke 22:1–6; John 18:1–11

Death and Resurrection of Jesus
Matthew 27—28; Mark 15—16; Luke 23—24:12; John 19:16—20:10

The risen Christ
Luke 24:35–49; John 20:19–23

Doubting Thomas
John 20:24–29

The Great Commission
Matthew 28:16–20

The Holy Spirit comes
Acts 2:1–4

Conversion of Saul
Acts 9:1–19

Peter is rescued from prison
Acts 12:6–10

Paul's missionary travels
Acts 13—21

Living for God
Romans 12

Love
1 Corinthians 13

The future
Revelation 21:1–8

Who's Who in the Bible
Old Testament

Adam and Eve

Adam and Eve are the parents of the human race. God created them to live in the Garden of Eden and be His friends. Eve disobeyed God and persuaded Adam to join her. Because they sinned, God sent them out of the garden. Sickness and death entered the world.

(Genesis 1:26—5:5)

Noah

Noah and his family were the only people God saved from the flood. God told Noah to build an ark and fill it with food for his family and with animals of every kind.

(Genesis 5:29—10:32)

Abraham and Sarah

Abraham and Sarah were the father and mother of God's people, the Jews. God promised Abraham that he would have more children than the stars in the sky. Abraham and Sarah were elderly and still had no children. Finally, God gave them a son named Isaac. God tested Abraham's faith many times, but Abraham trusted God.

(Genesis 11—25)

Isaac and Rebekah

Isaac was the son of Abraham and Sarah—the son God had promised them. He married Rebekah and God gave them twin sons. Rebekah told Jacob, the

This view of Noah's ark gives some indication of its massive dimensions.

younger son, to trick his father, Isaac, so he would get the family leadership. Jacob had to flee from Esau, his angry brother.

(Genesis 17:15—35:29)

Jacob and Rachel

Jacob the trickster was tricked by his uncle Laban into marrying Leah. Jacob had to work many years to marry Rachel, whom he loved. God changed Jacob's name to Israel. His sons and two grandsons became the twelve tribes of Israel.

(Genesis 25—50)

Joseph

Joseph was Jacob's best-loved son. His jealous brothers plotted to kill him, but instead they sold him into slavery. Joseph became the trusted slave of Pharaoh, an Egyptian leader. Later, he was accused of crimes, put in prison, and forgotten. Finally, Joseph was called to tell the meaning of a dream Pharaoh had. Overnight, Joseph became second to Pharaoh in all of Egypt. Because of famine, Joseph's brothers went to Egypt to buy food. They did not recognize their brother there. Joseph tested them, and when he found they were sorry for what they had done, he told them who he was.

(Genesis 30—50)

Moses

Moses was a Hebrew who grew up in Egypt, escaped to the desert, and returned to free God's people from slavery. The Egyptians did not want to lose their slaves, but after God sent ten plagues, they finally let them go. Moses had a difficult time leading the stubborn people, and they often disobeyed God. The short trip to the Promised Land became a forty-year journey. Moses was a strong leader who loved God and His people.

(Exodus, Leviticus, Numbers, and Deuteronomy)

Joshua

God chose Joshua to take Moses' place when he died. He was one of the twelve spies who went into the Promised Land. Joshua led the people into the Promised Land and during the battle of Jericho.

(Deuteronomy 1:22–40; Joshua 1—24)

Ruth

Ruth was not an Israelite; she was from the land of Moab. Her people prayed to idols, not to the true God. Ruth had married an Israelite in Moab. He, his brothers, and his father died. After their deaths, Naomi, Ruth's mother-in-law, was returning to Bethlehem. Ruth chose to go with Naomi and follow God. Ruth took care of her mother-in-law. God then gave Ruth a new husband, Boaz. God gave them a son named Obed, who was the grandfather of King David.

(Ruth 1—4)

Samuel

Samuel was a prophet and priest of the people of Israel. From boyhood, Samuel lived with Eli, the high priest. Samuel became a spiritual leader of his people and was the priest who anointed Saul as king, and later, David as well.

(1 Samuel 1—28)

Saul

Saul was the first king of Israel. At first, he obeyed God. Later, he disobeyed Him and Samuel said God would give the kingdom to someone else. Saul continued to reign for forty years. During much of that time, he chased David and tried to kill him. David waited patiently for God to give him the kingdom. Saul and his sons were killed on the same day in a battle with the Philistines.

(1 Samuel 9—31)

David

David was the best-known king of Israel. He became king after Saul was killed. The people loved David, which made Saul jealous. For many years before he became king, David had to flee from Saul. David was an excellent soldier, who learned his fighting skills from his years as a shepherd, fighting off lions and bears. Such knowledge helped him kill the powerful giant Goliath.

David also was a musician and poet. He played the harp and wrote many of the Psalms. People use his prayers and songs of praise to worship God today.

David loved God, but he still sinned. He truly was sorry and asked God to forgive him. God called David "a man after my own heart" (Acts 13:22).

(1 Samuel 16—31; 2 Samuel 1—24; 1 Kings 1—2)

Solomon

Solomon is known as the wisest man who ever lived. Solomon was the son of King David and Bathsheba and the third king of Israel. God allowed Solomon to build the Temple in Jerusalem where the Jewish people praised and worshiped God. It was famous for its beauty.

Solomon wrote many Proverbs, some Psalms, the Book of Ecclesiastes, and the Song of Songs in the Old Testament.

In spite of his wisdom, Solomon disobeyed God in a very important matter: he married many women from foreign countries, and his wives brought with them their idols. God divided Solomon's kingdom after he died.

(2 Samuel 12:24—24:25; 1 Kings 1:1—11:43)

Elijah

Elijah was a prophet so close to God that he never died; God took him straight to heaven. God let Elijah perform many important miracles. Elijah declared that there would be no rain until he said otherwise. Famine resulted. God used Elijah to bring a dead boy back to life.

Elijah took a bold stand against the prophets of Baal. King Ahab and Queen Jezebel were supporting Baal-worship. Elijah challenged all the prophets of Baal to prove who was the real God. Nothing happened when the priests of Baal prayed to their god, but when Elijah prayed to the Lord, He answered immediately.

(1 Kings 17:1—22:53; 2 Kings 1:1—2:11)

Ezra

Ezra was a faithful Jewish priest while he was a captive in Persia. King Artaxerxes allowed him to take other captives back to Jerusalem. They took with them things they needed to worship the Lord.

Ezra studied God's Law and taught the people, so they could repent and return to God.

(Ezra 1—10)

Esther

Esther is the second woman with a book of the Bible named after her. Esther was a young Jewish woman whom God used to save her people from being killed. She became queen to King Xerxes. A palace official plotted to kill all the Jews in Persia, but Queen Esther was able to expose the plan and save the Jews.

The Jewish holiday Purim is still celebrated in memory of that victory.

(Esther 1—10)

Job

Job is known for his patience. God allowed Satan to take away Job's wealth, family, and finally his health. Satan said Job served God only because he had an easy life, but God knew Job loved Him and not just the things God gave to him. Job did not understand why his life changed for the worse. Job's friends said he had done something wrong. Finally, Job realized God was even more powerful than he had thought. God gave Job new wealth and a new family.

(Job 1—42)

Isaiah

Isaiah was an Israelite who became a prophet when he saw a vision of the Lord in heaven. It made him very aware of his sinfulness to see God in all His holiness, but God forgave him and Isaiah was never the same after that. He faithfully preached that God was going to judge his people—but there was hope. Many of his prophecies are about the Messiah.

(Isaiah 1—66)

Jeremiah

Jeremiah warned his people about the punishment that God would send upon them, but they did not listen to him. They accused him of being a traitor. He was mocked and abused for preaching God's message, but he did not yield. Jeremiah was taken away into captivity along with the people from Jerusalem. He is called the weeping prophet because no one ever listened to him, and his people suffered the consequences at God's hands.

(Jeremiah 1—52; Lamentations 1—5)

Daniel

Daniel was a young Jewish man who became an adviser to four Babylonian kings while an exile in Babylonia. In Babylon, he prayed to God faithfully, even when he was in danger of losing his life by doing so. Once he was put into a den of hungry lions because he prayed to God, but God protected him and kept him alive.

God gave Daniel the ability to tell the meaning of dreams. He also prophesied about the end times.

(Daniel 1—12)

Jonah

Jonah was the prophet who tried to flee from God. He did not want to tell the wicked people of Nineveh to turn to God because he knew that God would forgive them if they did. It took a storm at sea and a rescue by a huge fish for Jonah to change his mind. Jonah finally did as God willed, but he never got past the fact that the people listened and were forgiven by God.

(Jonah 1—4)

New Testament

Mary

Mary, a young Jewish virgin, was chosen by God to conceive and bear His Son, Jesus Christ, by the power of the Holy Spirit. The angel Gabriel announced this to her in Nazareth. Mary stood at the foot of the Cross as Jesus died, and Jesus told the Apostle John to care for her. She was also in the upper room on the day of Pentecost.

(Matthew 1; Mark 6:3; Luke 1—2; John 2:1–11; 19:25–27; Acts 1)

John the Baptist

John the Baptist, son of Elizabeth and Zechariah, lived in the Judean wilderness. He wore clothes of camels' hair, as the prophet Elijah had done centuries earlier. He preached repentance, paving the way for his cousin Jesus whom he baptized in the River Jordan. John was imprisoned, and later beheaded, by Herod.

(Matthew 3; 11:1–19; 14:1–12; Mark 1:1–8; Luke 1; John 1:1–34)

Andrew

Andrew introduced his brother, Peter, to Jesus on the shores of Lake Galilee, where they, John, and James fished. Andrew brought to Jesus a boy who had two fish and five loaves, which Jesus used to feed 5,000 people.

(Matthew 4:18–20; Mark 1:16–18; John 1:35–42; 6:8–9)

Peter

Peter always heads the list of the Apostles. With his brother, Andrew, Peter left his fishing occupation and became one of Jesus' three closest Apostles. At Caesarea Philippi, he told Jesus He was "the Christ, the Son of the living God." Peter led the first Christians, preaching fearlessly from the day of Pentecost, when 3,000 people were baptized. Peter wrote two short letters, and much of Mark's Gospel is likely a summary of his teaching. He was executed by Nero in Rome.

(Matthew 4:18–20; 10:2; 14:25–31; 16:13–23; 17:1–13; 26:31–35, 69–75; 1 and 2 Peter)

Peter denies Jesus.

James

James was a fisherman, working with his brother, John, and father, Zebedee. Jesus called him, and he followed at once. Jesus gave John and James the nickname "sons of thunder." James became one of Jesus' three closest Apostles, whom Jesus chose to have with Him at special moments, such as the Transfiguration. James was beheaded for his Christian faith by Herod Agrippa I, about ten years after the death of Jesus.

(Matthew 4:21–22; 10:2; 17:1–13; 26:37; Mark 5:37; 10.35–45; Luke 9:51–56; Acts 12:2)

John

John, a fisherman and son of Zebedee, was one of Jesus' inner circle of three Apostles. John, who leaned on Jesus at the Last Supper, was Jesus' closest friend, and as Jesus was dying, He asked John to care for Mary, His Mother. John wrote one Gospel; the Book of Revelation, during his exile on the island of Patmos; and three short letters. In his

Gospel, John never mentions himself by name, but uses the words "the beloved disciple" instead. He became a leader in the early Church.

(Matthew 4:21–22; 10:2; 20:20–23; John 13:23–25; 19:25–27; Acts 1:13; 3–4; Galatians 2:9; 1, 2, and 3 John; Revelation 1:1)

Matthew

Matthew, also known as Levi, was called from being a tax collector to follow Jesus. He abandoned everything and held a feast in his house for Jesus and many tax collectors and sinners. He is the author of the first Gospel.

(Matthew 9:9–10)

Thomas

At the Last Supper, Thomas asked Jesus, "How can we know the way?" Jesus replied, "I am the way, and the truth, and the life." Thomas is remembered as "doubting" Thomas because he said he would never believe in Jesus' Resurrection unless he saw Jesus and touched His wounds. When the risen Lord Jesus did appear to him, Thomas immediately exclaimed, "My Lord and my God!"

(Matthew 10:3; John 11:16; 14:5–6; 20:24–28)

Philip

Philip was a fisherman from Bethsaida, who brought Nathanael (Bartholomew) to meet Jesus. At the Last Supper, Philip asked Jesus to show them the Father, and Jesus replied, "I am in the Father and the Father is in me."

(John 1:43–51; 6:5–7; 12:20–22; 14:8–9)

Judas Iscariot

Judas Iscariot was the treasurer for the Twelve Apostles. For thirty silver pieces, he betrayed Jesus in the Garden of Gethsemane. Judas was later overtaken by remorse, returned the silver, and hanged himself.

(Matthew 26:1— 27:10; Acts 1:15–26)

Mary Magdalene

Mary was named Magdalene after the town from which she came, Magdala. Jesus drove seven demons from her and she became His follower, standing close to His Cross when He died. Mary Magdalene was the first person Jesus appeared to after His Resurrection.

(Matthew 27:55–56; 28:1–10; Mark 15:40; 16:1–8; Luke 8:2; John 19:25; 20:1–18)

John Mark

Mark, or John Mark, writer of the second Gospel, lived in Jerusalem, where the first Christians met in his mother's house. Mark, cousin of Barnabas, accompanied Paul and Barnabas on their first missionary journey, but he left them halfway, and Paul refused to take him on his second journey. Later Mark joined Paul in Rome, and was described by Paul as "my son Mark." Mark's Gospel is based on Peter's account of Jesus' life related to John Mark.

(Mark; Acts 12–15; 2 Timothy 4; Philemon)

Mary

Mary, the sister of Martha and Lazarus, loved to sit at Jesus' feet and listen to His teaching. A short time before Jesus' death, she anointed His feet with perfume.

(Mark 14:3–9; Luke 10:38–42; John 11:1—12:8)

He asked Jesus many questions, but did not really understand His responses at first. Later on, he tried to defend Jesus before the religious authorities. The other leaders challenged him. After Jesus was crucified, Nicodemus helped Joseph of Arimathea bury Jesus. By then, he understood that Jesus is God's Son.

(John 3:1–21; 7:50–52; 19:39–40)

Martha

With her sister, Mary, and brother, Lazarus, Martha often entertained Jesus in her home in Bethany, near Jerusalem. Martha once complained to Jesus that Mary just sat and listened to Jesus while she did all the work. Jesus replied that Mary had chosen "the better part."

(Luke 10:38–42; John 11:1—12:8)

Luke

A Greek-speaking doctor who wrote the third Gospel, Luke was also a friend of Paul. He accompanied the Apostle on some of his journeys and recorded his experiences in the Acts of the Apostles. Luke sailed to Rome with Paul, staying with him while he was a prisoner there.

(Luke; Acts; Colossians 4; 2 Timothy 4)

Zacchaeus

Zacchaeus, a wealthy, fraudulent tax collector, climbed a tree to see Jesus as he passed through Jericho. Jesus told him to come down and then went to his house. Afterward, Zacchaeus called Jesus "Lord" and said he would give half his money to the poor.

(Luke 19)

Nicodemus

Nicodemus was a Jewish religious leader who went to talk with Jesus at night.

Barnabas

Barnabas was a Christian leader in the early Church. His name means "son of encouragement." The Apostles called him this because he always helped people. Once, he sold a piece of property and gave the money to help the needy.

Barnabas journeyed with Paul, taking the gospel to people who had not heard about Jesus.

(Acts 4:36–37; 9:27—15:39)

Stephen

Stephen was the leader of seven deacons the Jerusalem church chose to look after poor widows. Some Jews objected to Stephen's preaching. When he accused them of killing Jesus Christ, they stoned him to death. Stephen was the first Christian martyr. His death was witnessed by Saul (Paul).

(Acts 6:1—8:2)

Stephen is tried by the Jewish religious court.

247

Philip

Philip, along with Stephen, was one of seven deacons appointed by the Jerusalem church. He became a leading evangelist among the Samaritans and Gentiles and told a visiting Ethiopian official the Good News about Jesus, which resulted in the man's Baptism.

(Acts 6:5; 8:4–13, 26–40; 21:8)

Paul

Paul was a missionary, preacher, and writer of Scripture. God changed him from a man who hated Jesus and His followers to one of Jesus' most devoted Apostles. He took three missionary journeys to bring the gospel to places all over the Roman Empire.

People did not always like what he had to say. Paul was beaten, stoned, imprisoned, and harassed many times because of his love for Christ.

Thirteen letters of the New Testament are attributed to Paul: Romans, 1 Corinthians, 2 Corinthians, Galatians, Ephesians, Philippians, Colossians, 1 Thessalonians, 2 Thessalonians, 1 Timothy, 2 Timothy, Titus, and Philemon. In past centuries, it was thought that he was the author of a fourteenth letter, the Letter to the Hebrews, although this is now disputed.

(Acts 7:58—28:31 and the letters Paul wrote)

Silas

A leader of the church in Jerusalem, Silas went with Paul on his second missionary journey and was jailed with him at Philippi. Silas is probably the same as "Silvanus," mentioned in Paul's letters, and who helped Peter write his first letters.

(Acts 15—18; 2 Corinthians 1; 1 Thessalonians 1; 1 Peter 5)

Timothy

Timothy was like a son to the Apostle Paul. He went on missionary journeys with him. Paul also sent Timothy to help churches resolve difficulties. Timothy served some of these churches as pastor.

Paul wrote two Letters to Timothy, encouraging and instructing him in his duties. Timothy may have been with Paul when he died.

(Acts 16:1–5; Romans 16:21; Philippians 1:1)

Aquila and Priscilla

Aquila and Priscilla were a married couple who worked and journeyed with Paul. They were Jewish Christians from Rome who helped others understand the gospel. They opened their home as a church and made their living making tents.

(Acts 18; Romans 16:3—5; 1 Corinthians 16:19)

Index

Acknowledgments

Picture acknowledgments

Every effort has been made to trace and contact copyright owners. We apologize for any omissions or errors.

Illustrations

Fred Apps: pp. 22, 28, 76, 100, 104, 110, 115, 121, 136, 219, 244 (lion)

Shirley Bellwood: pp. 220, 231

Martin Bustamente: pp. 3/60–61/back cover, 3/102–03/back cover, 3/178–79/back cover, 64–65, 156–57/front cover inset, 160–61, 180–81, 186–87, 188–89

Bill Corbett: pp. 15/back gatefold, 26–27, 52–53/back cover, 150–51, 172–73/front gatefold, 196–97, 240

Peter Dennis: pp. 3/7, 3/195/front cover inset, 47/spine, 69 (bottom), 119, 126, 131, 159, 195, 208, 212, 233

Jeremy Gower: p. 44

Donald Harley: pp. 128 (top), 141, 203, 217

Alan Harris: pp. 29, 118

James Macdonald: p. 215

Tony Morris: pp. 152–53, 166–67

Alan Parry: pp. 24, 85, 105, 218

Alan Parry/© Bill Noller International Publishing, San Dimas, CA 91773: pp. 10, 14, 18 (bottom), 20, 21, 33, 34, 35, 41 (bottom), 42, 43, 50, 56, 57, 66, 91, 114, 132, 134, 165 (top), 168, 171, 174, 185, 210, 224, 225, 226

Claudia Saraceni: p. 140

Richard Scott: pp. 3/front cover inset (shadow of cross), 18 (top), 19, 23, 38, 40, 41 (top), 46 (both), 54, 58, 59, 69 (top), 82, 88, 93, 112 (bottom), 114, 145, 146 147/main cover illustration, 148, 149, 163 (both), 165 (bottom), 192, 214, 222, 241–43, 244 (Daniel), 245–47